Cover Letters!
Cover Letters!
Cover Letters!

2nd Edition

By
Richard Fein

CAREER PRESS
3 Tice Road
P.O. Box 687
Franklin Lakes, NJ 07417
1-800-CAREER-1
201-848-0310 (NJ and outside U.S.)
FAX: 201-848-1727

COVER LETTERS! COVER LETTERS! COVER LETTERS!
SECOND EDITION
ISBN 1-56414-262-0, $9.99
Printed in the U.S.A. by Book-mart Press

To order this title by mail, please include price as noted above, $2.50 handling per order, and $1.50 for each book ordered. Send to: Career Press, Inc., 3 Tice Road, P.O. Box 687, Franklin Lakes, NJ 07417.

Or call toll-free 1-800-CAREER-1 (NJ and Canada: 201-848-0310) to order using VISA or MasterCard, or for further information on books from Career Press.

Library of Congress Cataloging-in-Publication Data

Fein, Richard, 1946-
    Cover letters! cover letters! cover letters! / by Richard Fein. --
2nd ed.
        p.   cm.
    Includes index.
    ISBN 1-56414-262-0 (pbk.)
    1. Cover letters. 2. Job hunting.   I. Title.
HF5383.F365   1997
808'.06665--dc20
                                                            96-28345
                                                              CIP

Dedication

*To my parents, Harry and Celia,
my wife, Rhonda, and our children, Lauren and Gabrielle.
To my brother David, who should write more often.*

Acknowledgments

I would like to thank the following people who read portions of this book's manuscript and shared their comments with me. Of course, any errors of content, opinion or presentation remain strictly my own.

Denise Annatone, United States International University, Alexandra Bennett, Hamilton College, Patricia Bersmaier, Georgia Southern University, Ellen S. Bevan, University of Rochester, Mark Blackmer, MetLife, Rhonda Boyes, Trinity University, Colleen Capel, Wallace, Inc., David Clarkson, Arthur Andersen, LLP, Lydia Colon, Milwaukee Area Technical College, Linda Kent Davis, Brandeis University, Thomas Denham, Union College, Karin Dickie, Liberty Mutual, Jeanne Exline, University of Minnesota, Patrick Farrell, Jones College, William Fletcher, College of Mount St. Joseph, Jennifer Fujitani, Filene's, Bill Gerty, Heublein, Inc., William Gilinsky, Visicom, Inc., Michael Hirsch, GE Capital, Karin Hasking, University of Technology (Sydney, Australia), Mark Humphrey, GE Plastics, Lynett James, Randolph-Macon Women's College, Kathleen Kane, Stefan Agency of Northwestern Mutual Life, Pamela Graw Keiser, Bucknell University, Judity A.D. Kennedy, Travelers Insurance, Drew Langevin, Providian Bancorp, John Lentine, Rex Lumber Company, Valerie Lipow, Career Counselor/Consultant, Marcia Merrill, Loyola College in Maryland, Maureen Pernick, Canisius College, John Polumbo, Polumbo & Partners, LLP, Eileen Quaglino, Ramapo College of New Jersey, Larry Sechney, Kutztown University, R. Michael Shaldone, New York Life Insurance Company, Dawn Scheffner, Northern Illinois University, Trish Shafer, SmithKline Beecham, Jack Stewart, Abilene Christian University, Gerri Sullivan, Youngstown State University, Lisa Sullivan, Andersen Consulting, Lisa Tarsi, Millsaps College, Ian Walsh, Data General, Dale Zeretzke, The Dolphin Group, Robert Zikell, Digital Equipment Corporation

In addition, I would like to thank my assistant Janice Dagilus, without whom my work life would be impossible; Betsy Sheldon, my editor, and Ron Fry, my publisher.

Richard Fein
December, 1996

Contents

Introduction

••

Why You Need
This Book

••

This book is for the person who can *do* a good job, but needs some help in *landing* one. You might be an individual who has been working for a number of years and is now seeking new employment, someone returning to the full-time job market, or a new college graduate. As a career specialist for 16 years, I will share with you the approaches that have helped other job-seekers succeed in any economic climate.

My central topic is cover letters, a necessary element of most job searches. You will learn how to write a cover letter that is a powerful tool in obtaining a good job and not simply required baggage on top of your resume. Because this book is for thinking people, I will show you the process of writing a good cover letter (or any job-related letter for that matter), in addition to giving you a variety of samples. By using this book, you will write your own successful letters, rather than trying to copy from others.

You will also learn how to do efficient research on industries, firms and jobs. That research will help you succeed in three ways. First, you will be able to link your strengths to the needs of prospective employers. Second, you will be able to send out thoughtful, targeted letters using the modular construction technique I will show you. Third, you will express your motivation in a way that tells a firm that you are seriously interested in them.

Why a second edition?

The first edition of *Cover Letters! Cover Letters! Cover Letters!* came out in 1994. It was exceptionally well-received, and generated hundreds of calls, letters, comments and even suggestions for additions to the book. Thus, we have updated, expanded and added new topics that you've asked us to cover, specifically:

- We have added 30 new or updated cover letter examples.
- We have expanded several chapters to discuss computerized job search in general and its impact on your cover letter in particular.

Basic premise

You may be wondering about my basic premise. After all, aren't the odds stacked against you when you submit an unsolicited cover letter and resume? Isn't networking really the way to go? The answer to both questions is yes—but only partially so.

You may have read that the success rate (securing interviews) is between 3 to 5 percent for unsolicited interview requests. Don't let those figures frighten you. Even assuming those figures are correct, remember:

- Most job-search campaigns are sadly deficient. They are nondirected and supported by poor cover letters and resumes. This book will show you how to write an excellent cover letter as part of a directed campaign. That should increase your success rate significantly.

- Let's be pessimistic for a moment. Assume that you sent out 100 cover letters with only a 3-percent to 5-percent success rate. The result is three to five interviews you would not have had otherwise.

- Networking is important to help you gain a better understanding of different employment situations and to uncover job leads. We will devote an entire chapter to this subject. However, more often than not, a new job lead must be followed up by a cover letter and resume. So networking increases the opportunities to use a good cover letter; it does not eliminate the need for them.

- Good cover letters will help you secure interviews in the large labor market represented by small businesses. Chapter 12 will show you how to access the sometimes elusive small business job market.

- Even when they are not required, cover letters can help you secure interviews. One example would be as a follow-up to employers you might meet at a job fair.

Many people feel anxious about writing anything. When a job is at stake, anxiety can reach panic levels. However, by following the modular construction approach presented in this book, you can channel your energy of writer's panic into producing an effective letter.

Why a resume isn't enough

Perhaps you are wondering if you should rely on a well-written resume to secure job interviews for yourself. Resumes are important—in partnership with your cover letter. In fact, your cover letter can be more valuable to you than a resume. With a modest amount of effort, cover letters can be tailored to address specific employment situations. Cover letters can also tell particular employers about your motivation. In principle, resumes can be adapted to varying situations, too. However, the process is more difficult and most people won't write a new resume for each of dozens, let alone hundreds, of prospective employers.

●●

Most of the examples given in this book are of individuals who are not obvious candidates for the kind of position they are seeking. That is, like most job-seekers, they are looking to change firms, industries or even careers. If your current job situation is not very similar to the new situation you are seeking, your cover letter is especially important. First, it must demonstrate the positive characteristics you have that the next employer needs. Second, your letter must express an articulated motivation for wanting the new job. This book will show you how to write cover letters that make candidates who are not obvious into the ones who win the job interviews.

●●

A cover letter offers you a chance to present yourself in a way that will appeal directly to each employer. That is, you will be able to link your talents to the needs of a particular situation. In addition you will be able to articulate your motivation for wanting to work for that particular employer. This combination will make you shine above scores of others pursuing the same job. By showing you how to write a good cover letter, this book will help you obtain a competitive advantage in today's tough labor market.

Computerized data submission and your cover letter

In the last several years, a good deal of attention has been focused on the computer applicant processing now in use by many firms. Some people have assumed erroneously that this innovation reduces the need for cover letters. This book includes an entire chapter to address the issue and adds new information in other chapters as well.

Electronic job search techniques are a new tool in your hands, not a club over your head. Your cover letter remains critical to your job search. How to construct your cover letter has changed in some cases, however, and this is illustrated in the new edition. See Chapter 7 and Chapter 9.

For most people, the really significant change is in the resources available to you in organizing your job hunt research. Chapter 2, Chapter 7, Chapter 9 and Chapter 12 have been updated to include this new resource.

Meet the Job Search Club

This book is written through the experiences of a "Job Search Club" (JSC). The members are composites of people with whom I have worked over the years. The Job Search Club format makes presenting the process of cover-letter writing easier to understand and a discussion of applying successful principles to different situations more meaningful. In your own job search, you may wish to work with a small group or as an individual, depending on your own preferences and circumstances.

There are eight members in our Job Search Club. Five are experienced workers, but inexperienced in looking for a job. Three are recent college graduates.

Gabrielle: She is returning to the professional labor market after having spent a number of years raising her children. What does she need to restart her career? How will she avoid dead-end jobs?

●●●●●●●●●●●●

Cecily: She has worked at the same firm for years. Now the firm is downsizing. She never had to look for work before—what does she do now?

Anthony: After working in the same position for five years, it's time for a move. Where does he go next and how does he get there?

Harry: Like Anthony, he is a seasoned professional, but unlike Anthony, Harry wants to change fields, not progress in his current one.

Lauren: She has seen the corporate life and may want to apply her talents to a nonprofit organization. Are there any pitfalls?

David, Jeannette and Bill are recent college graduates looking for their first professional job. How do you get a job when everyone seems to want experience? David majored in liberal arts, Jeannette in business, Bill in engineering. How will their majors affect the way they write their cover letters?

We will see how the same cover letter principles apply to each Job Search Club member, but we will also see how the application changes to meet differing circumstances.

How this thinking person's book is organized

This book is organized to present the process of writing a good cover letter in manageable parts. The first section explains why a cover letter is necessary and how to conduct enough research to write a letter with impact.

In the second section, we will look at the four paragraphs of a good cover letter—one at a time. We will learn the principles involved, and the reasons for them, by examining drafts written by Job Search Club members. The next logical step is polishing your product—the topic of our third section. We will see the JSC write several cover letters and discuss ways to improve them. Then we will work with a prototype letter. Using modular construction, we will see how to turn a prototype into dozens of cover letters. Then I will show you how to make your cover letter a partner that adds value to your resume and doesn't just repeat it.

In the last section, we will see how to organize your outreach effort. This includes sample cover letters representing different situations, a step-by-step approach to networking and developing a strategy for your job search that will include the growing labor market of small firms.

The appendix will give you some helpful references for your job search and some hints on writing better by writing tighter.

Writing a good cover letter may seem like a difficult task. However, your cover letter will play a large role in determining whether you obtain a job you really want or just fall into something you managed to get. As the retold tale of the fisherman explains, the task is difficult, but using this book will make it doable.

A fisherman's tale: Don't get hooked on the worms

Career specialists like to tell the tale of the fisherman's advice to his children: "Give a person a fish and they will eat for a day. Teach that person how to fish, and they can eat for a lifetime."

The fisherman's advice is sound. People today tend to change jobs six or more times in the course of their career. Since getting a job is not a once-in-a-lifetime event, learning how to get a job is critical. But let's retell the story as it relates to this book:

The fisherman: Based on my years of experience, I am ready to teach you how to fish, John.

John: Save the lesson. Just give me a fish! I'm too hungry. Besides, after all the work I put in on my job and in college before that, I deserve it.

The fisherman: Sorry, John, the world doesn't owe you a living any more than it owes it to anyone else.

John: Maybe so. But I don't like worms and hooks.

The fisherman: That's understandable. Worms and hooks may seem like a burden to you, but I will show you how to use them as tools for your own advantage. Then you will be able to catch a wide variety of fish whenever you feel it's time to change your diet.

Chapter 1

Cover Letters: Who Needs Them

In this chapter, we will find out why cover letters are so important to a successful job search. Then we will learn how your cover letter can add value to your resume.

The Job Search Club talks with a corporate recruiter

It was 6 p.m. and time for me to lead another session of our Job Search Club. Our members came from varying circumstances, but we all had one goal in common: to take a step forward in our careers by moving to a new job. We were able to come together because the basic principles of a good job search held true for all of us. At the same time, we would discuss the differing application of those principles to the varying circumstances of our JSC members.

Today we were beginning a series of workshops on cover letters. We were fortunate to have Rhonda Jamieson from Dollarco present to share her experiences as a corporate recruiter. As usual, we opened up with questions. Lauren, who was looking for a new job after five years with the same employer, wasn't shy about jumping right in.

Lauren: We're going to be spending a number of sessions on cover letters. Why? Any employer we are interested in will get our resume. It seems to me that should be enough. So why bother with cover letters?

Rhonda: There are three basic reasons: First, it is expected. An unsolicited resume by itself, sometimes called a naked resume, isn't very likely to be read. Because the cover letter is a bit of a hassle, having one has become a screening mechanism in itself. Second, a good cover letter will add value to your resume, increasing the chances you'll get a positive response. Third, your cover letter is an example of your written communication, a critical skill in today's working world.

Gabrielle: I don't like hurdles for the heck of it, but I can live with the first reason you gave. It's your second point that troubles me. If your resume is well-written, what value can the cover letter add?

Value added: critical means to a necessary end

Rhonda: That's a good question, Gabrielle. The cover letter adds to your attractiveness as a candidate in three ways.

Highlighting: You can give those positive characteristics of greatest interest to a particular employer more prominence in the cover letter than you did in your resume.

Reframing: Through your cover letter, you can put some of your experiences in a frame of reference that more closely meets the needs of the employer.

New material: Your cover letter can include material of interest to an employer that would be difficult to present in a resume. Your motivation for wanting to work for that particular company is an example.

I understand from Richard that you will see examples of these points as you work on your cover letters.

(David, a graduating college senior, carried us forward by asking the next logical question.)

David: Is there anything special about cover letters for recent or forthcoming college graduates?

Rhonda: Cover letters are more important for college seniors for two reasons. First, students lack the immediate credibility of someone advancing within a profession. After all, the college senior's positive characteristics probably weren't demonstrated in jobs like the one you want to get. You probably couldn't have a job like the one you want without your degree, but that doesn't change this reality.

Second, there is a common perception, often an accurate one, that "young people these days just don't know what they want." You need to convince the employer that you do have a sense of direction based on a well-thought-out interest in a particular career field. Giving specifics is critical to demonstrating a credible interest.

Specifics and credibility

Rhonda has made an important point. Compare these statements for yourself:

Jan: I have always had an interest in your products. Furthermore, working for a fine company like yours would be just what I am looking for.

Fran: There are two reasons for my interest in Firmco. First, I am convinced from my research that your main product, the self-opening envelope, has the potential to capture a large share of the stationery market. Second, I am impressed by a recent article in *Inc.* magazine that referred to your firm as one "destined to grow straight into the 21st century." Since I want to grow with an innovative company, Firmco seems to be a good place to build a career.

Jan's statement sounds like generic fluff that she could say to anyone. Does Jan even know anything about Firmco? Fran shows she has taken the time to research Firmco and has related her understanding of the firm to her own goals.

I would interview Fran. Any takers for Jan?

• •

David pressed Rhonda a bit more on how she, as a corporate recruiter, would read a cover letter before determining whether to invite someone to an interview. Rhonda reflected for a moment before giving a response she called the "triumphant trilogy."

The triumphant trilogy

Rhonda: There are three key questions I ask myself when I receive a cover letter. First, does s/he have what we need? If the writer lets me know that s/he has several positive characteristics we need, I am impressed. Most people have many positive characteristics. But it is your responsibility to identify several that are important to us. If you do, that is a strong reason to take you seriously.

Second, why is this person writing to us? We get plenty of job applications, but most seem to know nothing about us. You will stand out above them if you can let me know what it is about working specifically for us that's appealing to you. Similarly, I like to see in a cover letter that you have a realistic sense of direction in your career. Otherwise, all you are saying is "Help, I need a job."

Third, can you communicate in writing? Communication is a critical skill in any business today. My counterparts in the nonprofit sector will tell you the same thing. Your cover letter is presumably an example of your written communication at its best. Therefore, if you write well, I am more likely to want to see you.

Lauren: Rhonda, how long do you spend reading a typical cover letter?

Rhonda: Usually less than a minute. Sometimes a lot less.

David: That's awful! I just spent four years in college, and we get maybe a minute with our cover letter?

Lauren: It's even more awful for me. After five years of hard work, I deserve more attention than that!

Rhonda: That is the reality, awful or not. Besides, it is not so harsh as it may seem. If you have something attractive to tell us, you can usually get it across in a minute or less. If you have nothing to say, or you just can't deliver the message quickly, you haven't earned an interview anyway.

Before Rhonda left, she gave each JSC member a chart summarizing her advice. See page 17.

The credibility gap

We thanked Rhonda for her time and insights. Then we discussed more questions on the minds of the Job Search Club members.

Gabrielle: Based on what Rhonda said, one key issue we need to consider is establishing credibility.

Richard: Credibility—namely, the quality that says I can believe what I read, see or hear—is important. We need to address that issue head-on.

Let's construct a chart to identify reasons for the credibility problem and ways to address it. Everyone faces one or more of these problems:

Credibility gap chart

Problem	Solution
Lacks the credibility of similar professional experience.	I know what you need that I can offer; I will give you examples to support my positive characteristics.
Common belief that you lack a career focus; you don't know what you really want.	I will tell you at least three things I want in a job that I can find working for you.
Concern that you won't adjust to a new environment.	I will give an example of flexibility, previous adapting to a new environment or exposure to a similar work environment.
You will want to take a bow instead of moving on to the next act. (Some talented people feel that they have somehow earned their place in a job because of good performance in the past. In reality your good performance in the past is valuable mainly as a predictor of good performance in the future.)	I will make it clear that I am excited about the possibility of a new opportunity and will work hard to succeed.

In short, you can establish credibility in two ways: first, by linking your talents and wants to the firm's needs and characteristics; second, by supporting your statements with good examples. We will be working on both those points in the next few meetings of the Job Search Club.

Easy pieces

Lauren wondered out loud if the task of writing a cover letter was just too large to do well. I told her that we would learn how to write good cover letters by dividing the task into easy pieces:

- Research (Chapter 2).
- Four paragraphs in a cover letter. These are discussed in Chapters 3, 4, 5 and 6.

Approached that way, once we've done our basic research and drafted a prototype cover letter, individual letters to specific employers should take about 20 minutes to write.

Rhonda's advice to the JSC

A cover letter gives the employer	Particular importance to your job search
Positive Characteristics: Do you offer the qualities the firm needs in a new employee? What have you demonstrated, achieved or learned that would benefit a new employer?	If you are *remaining in the same profession* but changing employers, the very context of your experience lends credibility. However, you still want to tie your positive characteristics to the prospective employer's needs. If you are seeking a more responsible position, a sentence or two showing specific talents needed for promotion would be helpful. If you are *a recent graduate*, your work experience probably was not directly in the field you wish to enter. So, it is especially important to clearly identify three positive characteristics of importance to a particular situation, even if those characteristics developed outside a work environment. If you are *returning to the work force*, you need to re-establish credibility by demonstrating that you understand what the employer needs. In all cases, each positive characteristic should be validated by giving an example of where you demonstrated, achieved or learned it.
Motivation and direction: Why are you writing to that specific company in connection to a particular kind of job? Do you have a realistic sense of where you are going	"Why do you want to work for us?" is one of the great questions of the job search process. Unless you provide an answer, a firm will likely believe that you're just looking for a job. You want to show your particular interest in them. Identify reasons why you are attracted to that company and why you are seeking a particular kind of job.
Communication: Can you communicate in writing?	Communication is a critical skill in today's work world. Presumably, your cover letter is an example of your written communication at its best. All job applicants should be careful to show that they can communicate in a clear, to-the-point manner.
Value added: Your cover letter adds value to your resume by: highlighting, reframing and introducing new material.	For most job-seekers, their resume alone will not clearly address how their positive characteristics will be useful in a new situation or what motivates them to seek a particular work situation. The cover letter can supply the missing pieces.

Is there a quantity/quality tradeoff?

David asked a question about the quantity/quality tradeoff in letter-writing: "Given the difficult current job market, I feel that I want to send out a large number of resumes," David began. "On the other hand, I know that a high-quality letter is important to securing an interview. The time required for a quality letter would seem to conflict with writing a lot of them and vice-versa. Is there a way out of this dilemma?"

I told David that I understood his concern. There is a tradeoff of sorts, but we will learn how to minimize your problems with it. You will develop a good prototype letter while building an inventory of your positive characteristics and research findings. Once you learn how to amend your prototype with material from your inventory, you will be able to write high-quality cover letters in significant quantities. In combination with the well-designed outreach campaigns we will organize, you will be able to maximize your chances for success.

What is a prototype?

Harry, who is considering a change in career direction, followed up on David's question.

Harry: We have mentioned a "prototype" cover letter several times. What do you mean by a "prototype" anyway?

Richard: Each member of the JSC is going to develop a cover letter that includes all the key points we have been discussing. That letter can be quickly amended for different situations using the inventories we will build in the course of our research. That's what makes it a prototype—a solid, basic letter that can become many different letters with a limited amount of thoughtful changes.

Not the great American novel

Lauren rejoined the discussion. "I want to be proud of what I write," she told us. "If my name is going on something, it had better be my best." Lauren had certainly made a good point, and I told her so. At the same time, I suggested to her, "best" has to be put in context. For a cover letter, "best" means the best you can do given the constraints you are under (time, energy) and the goal you want to achieve. So your best cover letter is the one that gives you the best chance of securing a job interview without driving yourself crazy in the process.

Lauren wasn't completely satisfied. "But how will I know for sure that I have done the right things in the right way?" she asked.

••

What does it mean "to know"?

Lauren's question is central to carrying out a job-search campaign. How do we know what to put in a resume or cover letter, what to say at an interview, to whom we should send our correspondence?

The answer is, we don't. Not in the absolute sense of knowing that 2+2=4 or that Abraham Lincoln was born on February 12. Knowing in our context means doing what will bring the highest probability of success based on our best reasonable efforts to identify the best available information. We try to increase our probabilities, realizing that sometimes we will not succeed. This is more effective than investing an inordinate amount of time and energy in an elusive pursuit of knowing for certain.

• •

Gabrielle: At first I thought I would have nothing to say. Now I see I may have too much to say. Why not really strut my stuff and give them two or three pages of interesting material?

Richard: Yes, you do have a lot you could say and I am glad you recognize that. But your task is to identify the most important items to convey to the reader. If you go beyond one page, you are making two mistakes:

1. You are conveying your inability to establish priorities and communicate effectively. That is the opposite of what you want to do.

2. A long letter may be too time-consuming for a prospective employer to read at all.

Who knows where the time goes?

David asked what everyone was thinking: "This sounds like a lot of work. Okay, the cover letter is necessary, but let's be realistic. Will we have the time and energy to do it right?"

I told David that we would develop an approach to cover letters that would make writing them doable at a reasonable cost in time and energy. In the process, we would actually increase our job opportunities in two ways. First, it would make a successful outreach campaign possible. That is, you will be able to take the initiative in contacting employers of interest to you. Second, the process you use for writing your cover letters will help you interview better as well.

Where will the time come from? Let's assume that you're just starting your job search, so you'll need a lot of time researching and gathering your materials. At the same time, let's assume that your work or academic commitment consumes 10 hours a day, Monday through Friday.

The basic research the Job Search Club carries out takes a total of about 10 hours. Once it's complete, it is available to you and doesn't need to be repeated. Networking, which we discuss in Chapter 11, may consume one hour per meeting, including contact letters and follow-up. Your prototype cover letter will take about three hours to write. Once it is written you will want to change it, but you won't have to start from scratch. Changes to your prototype to suit different circumstances will take about 20 minutes per letter in the beginning and even less as you grow more skilled.

The standard week has 168 (7 x 24) hours, of which you need to sleep about 56 (7 x 8). We assume about 21 hours a week for eating (3 x 7) and 50 hours for work or academics. That leaves you 41 hours per week open after taking care of necessities. If you take just half of that time and divide it between networking and outreach letters, you could have 10 networking meetings a week and send out at least 60 letters.

Voltaire's axiom

The famous French philosopher once said, "If I only had time to write, I would write you a short letter." Long letters tend to ramble and hide the main points. Do the employer—and yourself—a favor. Keep it short.

Where do we go from here?

In this chapter, the Job Search Club learned that cover letters are a necessary part of an outreach campaign. However, your cover letter should be seen as an asset, not a burden. It adds value to your resume, increasing your chances of getting the interviews you want.

In the next chapter, we will take an important step: *Organizing Research.*

Chapter 2

∙∙∙

Organizing Research

∙∙∙

In this chapter, we will learn how to organize job-search research by following the activities and thought processes of Job Search Club members. Then the JSC members will learn how to build inventories to make the information they find readily accessible for their cover letters. This research effort should take between six and 10 hours. The result will be more interviews and a better job.

The important part of this chapter is the research process it describes. The steps JSC members take in researching a particular career, industry or firm provide an example of how you can research any career, industry or firm.

Why your research is important

The Job Search Club gathered for its regular meeting with a sense of anticipation. This week we were going to start the research we could use in a multitude of cover letters. Those cover letters would be used in an outreach campaign—namely, contacting employers on our own initiative. Later we talked about identifying the names of possible employers (See Chapter 12).

I invited the JSC members to discuss their concerns. Anthony spoke up first.

Anthony: How will doing the research you suggest help us?

Richard: Your research will help you in two ways:

1. You will be able to write cover letters that will show you have the characteristics each particular employer wants and a well-articulated motivation for writing. That will give you an advantage over your competitors in the job market.

2. You will be able to identify more employers who might be of interest to you.

David: Personally, I am getting a little antsy. It's a tough job market out there. I want to get something moving right away. Why do all this research before we even have an interview scheduled?

Richard: I can certainly understand your feeling. You want to jump right in and start interviewing. In fact, it may be possible for a college student like you to get some interviews through an on-campus recruiting program. But you want to land the best job possible. That means looking beyond the recruiters who visit your college, just as experienced workers shouldn't just sit around waiting for a headhunter to call. Your research will help you cast a stronger, wider net to catch more of the fish you want—namely, job opportunities. In addition, what we learn here will help you prepare for job interviews as well.

Gabrielle: This whole idea of researching for an outreach campaign bothers me. Even with our best efforts, we will end up contacting firms that won't interview us or anyone else for that matter.

Richard: Good point, Gabrielle. You will get lots of no's. The only way to avoid that is not to look for a job at all. But the result of your research will be well-written, well-directed cover letters. That will significantly increase the probability of getting more yes's.

Lauren: I have worked hard for five years to make a mark in my firm. When I graduated college in 1988, I landed this position right away, even though I had very little experience. Now I've got to work hard just to get a new job. It isn't fair!

Richard: All your hard work will pay off twice for you, Lauren. First, it has helped you progress with your current employer. Second, because your hard work has produced results, you will be more attractive to a new employer. What you achieved yesterday will make your job search easier tomorrow.

Born in the wrong year?

The 1990s are tougher than the mid- to late 1980s for finding a job. That is a sad reality we all must accept. But none of us individually is going to change the economy. Put your energy into what you can influence: how hard and how well you look for a good job. About 110 million Americans are working, so there are jobs out there. It is within your power to land a good one for yourself.

After we addressed the JSC's general concerns, we moved to some more pragmatic questions. Harry opened this part of our discussion: "How can we organize our research so that we can write many cover letters without starting from scratch each time?" We discussed Harry's question and identified three areas for immediate research:

- Career/job.
- Industry/products.
- Specific company.

Of these three points, the first two can be researched for a whole cluster of potential companies. For example, if you are interested in commercial banking, letters to all commercial banks of interest could draw upon the same industry research. If you are interested in being a retail buyer, letters to all retailers could draw upon the same career research. Only information specific to a given firm would require its own research. Even then, we will see how company-specific research, too, can be conducted to benefit letters for more than one firm.

It was time to start our research, so three JSC members were assigned a topic and asked to report back to the group. David was assigned to identify sources of information about different careers.

What do they pay you for?

David undertook his assignment with relish. Although he was very bright, he didn't really have a clear picture of what people did for a living outside of his own experiences. What sources could he use to learn about a career?

David believed in basics first. He looked in the reference catalog in his town's main library under "Careers." He saw a number of citations, but this one really caught his eye:

Encyclopedia of Careers & Vocational Guidance
J. G. Fergusen Publishing

When David looked over the four volumes of the encyclopedia, he was pleasantly surprised. It was well-organized, very informative and interesting. "That's three-for-three on my list of desirability," David thought to himself. The steps David took would apply to most careers. However, he had been assigned market research, so David looked under that title. These are the headings David saw:

- Definition.
- History of the Field.
- Nature of the Work.
- Requirements.
- Special Requirements.
- Opportunities for Experience & Exploration.
- Related Occupations.
- Methods of Entering.
- Advancement.
- Employment Outlook.
- Earnings.
- Conditions of Work.
- Social and Psychological Factors,
- Sources of Additional Information.

David quickly skimmed the whole article and then pulled a small stack of 5" x 8" file cards from his briefcase. "I'm going to write down 10 or 12 key pieces of information," he thought to himself. "I'll use a separate file card for each key idea. That way, the information will be more easily accessible when I need it."

David began to take his notes following the encyclopedia's outline. He decided to write whole sentences or just key words based on two considerations: time and future usefulness. These are the notes David took on his file cards:

1. "The marketing research personnel collect, analyze and interpret data to determine potential sales of a product or service." [Key actions: reports, recommends preferences/costs/distribution/advertising.]

2. Statistical emphasis grew in the 1930s and 1940s.

3. Four basic jobs: statistician, project supervisor, coder, field interviews. Heavy use of questionnaires.

4. Requirements: "Intelligent, facile w/words & numbers, problem-solving re: data collection & data analysis. Don't need a license."

5. Related occupations: ad agency workers, economists, public relations, sales (including promotions), statisticians.

6. Methods of entering: contacts through professors, friends, relatives, summer employment.

7. Usually begin as junior analysts or research assistants.

8. 29,000 employed full-time in 1990. Expected to grow because of increased competition among producers.

9. Usually work a standard 40-hour week. (David made a note for himself to see if a 40-hour week was still true).

10. "Persons who enjoy variety & change will find 'new problems & new faces' aspect of market research most satisfying." Reality of tight deadlines.

David noted that several professional associations were listed as sources of additional information. "I'll call or write each one," he said. "Maybe they can send me some literature about their field and/or suggest a useful bibliography."

Obviously, David wasn't going to wait around until he received some literature in the mail. "What else could I be looking at in the meantime?" he asked himself. David knew that, like many colleges, libraries had a SIGI Plus computer software program available to use. He decided to check it out.

SIGI Plus

David's local library had a computer software package called SIGI Plus, a product of the Educational Testing Service located in Princeton, New Jersey. (If SIGI Plus is not available to you, a similar product may be found in your college or local library.) David hadn't used SIGI Plus before, so he read the instruction brochure next to the computer. He noticed that the program was comprised of eight separate sections, each of which looked valuable. However, the most directly useful section for his current purpose was called "Skills."

David was pleased that SIGI Plus was easy to use ("If you can boot up the computer, you're in business," he remarked) and allowed him to proceed at his own pace. The "Skills" section guides users in identifying what skills (the JSC would use the more inclusive term "positive characteristics") a particular occupation required, how that skill would be used in the profession and whether the user felt s/he had that skill. This information could be obtained simply by inputting a three-digit code for that profession and following the step-by-step guidance of the SIGI Plus program.

"Let me work through market research and see what I can learn," David said to himself. He typed in the three-digit code for market research and found that the program summarized about 10 skills as being important in that field. One of these skills was "making presentations." David wanted to learn more about that skill first because he enjoyed making presentations in his local civic organization. This is the information that came up on the SIGI Plus screen:

• •

"Uses statistics, graphs and tables to present results of consumer opinion poll to company management; presents set of recommendations to improve product image among customers."

• •

"That's interesting. I used statistics and graphs when I made my report to the League of Women Voters on local voting participation in the 1996 presidential election. Last year, I presented my recommendations for our 'Helping the Homeless' campaign. I never thought my community involvement would find such a direct application in a potential career," David said to himself. "Let me check out the description of the other skills discussed in this section."

David went beyond just collecting information. He thought about how to apply what he learned to himself. To make his research and self-reflection available for later use, he developed a chart like the one on page 26. Notice how David usually found an example of where he had demonstrated, achieved or learned a skill even though he had never been a market researcher. Similarly, many people have skills needed in a particular profession, even though they may have acquired that skill in a different context.

Combining his research in the *Encyclopedia of Careers & Vocational Guidance,* his exploration through SIGI Plus and his own self-reflection, David now had gained these assets for pursuing a job in marketing research:

- A sense of the field and its related occupations.
- A knowledge of what skills were needed in the field.
- Examples of where David had demonstrated, achieved or learned these skills in the past.

(In Chapter 11, we'll see how David explored another possible career by asking people in the profession about their jobs.)

Researching an industry

Harry was assigned to explore sources for a given industry or set of products. The steps Harry took in his research would be applicable to most industries or products. In his particular case, Harry decided to research consumer edibles (and drinkables): "I love food and everyone has to eat. Personal interest and career opportunities might combine, at least in terms of this project." Harry established his criteria for a good source to start with:

- Easily accessible.
- Informative.
- Intelligible to a nonexpert.

The first book in the library's reference section to meet Harry's criteria was:

Standard & Poor's
Industry Surveys
Standard & Poor's Corporation

Marketing research (based on SIGI Plus)

Skill	Use in the Profession	David's Example of Demonstration, Achievement or Learning
Advising	Advise management about ways to improve public's view of company's products; advise management about potential market for new products.	1. Advised freshman on how to survive first year at Emeritus.
Supervisory	Supervise interviewers, editors and coders involved in research project; make sure that answers to survey questions are accurately recorded.	1. Supervised junior counselors at overnight camp.
Making Presentations	Use statistics, graphs and tables to present results of consumer opinion poll to company management; present set of recommendations to improve product image among consumers.	1. Praised by professors for both content & delivery of classroom presentations. 2. Presented plan to abolish poverty to the student senate.
Writing	Phrase survey questions clearly and coherently; select set of questions to find out whether company's advertisement is successful in reaching consumers; write detailed report on findings of research project.	1. Wrote recommendations to improve customer service after a summer job. 2. Wrote both brief & extended term papers.
Keeping records; cataloging	Code answers to consumer opinion survey to make them conform to established measure; keep file of statistical and behavioral data on consumer buying pattern.	1. This one is tougher. Maybe I could mention my record-keeping of facts I used in term papers.
Gathering information, conducting research	Determine potential sales volume in geographical area on request of company's marketing executives; collect and study data on competition's pricing policies, distribution techniques and buying incentives.	1. I've done tons of research for college, but maybe a better example could be drawn from my research for the "Stop Pollution" committee.
Making Diagrams	Prepare diagrams to illustrate presentation to company management; plot consumers' responses on diagram; plot growth of product's sales against consumers' income brackets.	1. Drew diagrams indicating budget sources; voting patterns.
Analyzing, Interpreting, Evaluating	Evaluate effectiveness of company's advertising campaign; conduct survey designed to find reasons behind recent plunge of product's sales figures; spot trends in consumer buying habits.	1. Analyzed data on voting patterns among vegetarians. Interpreted results as indicating "Give me your beef" was a poor slogan for this group. Evaluated alternative approaches.
Analyzing Numerical Data	Study statistical data to find correlation between family income and demand for company's product; analyze results of survey to forecast consumers' response to company's new product; evaluate statistical significance of responses to questionnaire.	1. I'm not a math whiz, but I have analyzed data in both sociology & political science classes. Actually, given the importance of demographics to market research, these classes might be a good context for an example.
Working with computers	Use electronic data processing equipment to process and analyze information obtained in telephone interviews; use statistical software packages to perform multivariate regression analysis on results of consumer polls.	1. I've used some packages, but I can't really program.

The handy Standard & Poor's reference contained at least several pages of information about hundreds of industries. Harry saw that under "Food" there was a separate entry for "Beverages." Harry looked under "Beverages" and noted that this category was further divided into alcoholic and nonalcoholic. "That's an important distinction," Harry thought to himself. "Given my values, I really couldn't work for a beer or wine company. Besides, the nonalcoholic beverage industry is big enough for this project. I will narrow my research to nonalcoholic beverages." The reference book had about three pages on that topic.

The first thing Harry noted was that soda sales (the carbonated subset of non-alcoholic beverages) were flattening out and that "a continued slowdown is likely...attributable to changing lifestyles and purchasing patterns..." "This would make my plans to change to that career more difficult," Harry thought to himself. "I should keep it in mind as I develop my job-search strategy."

The article went on to discuss the spirited competition for market share, with Dr. Pepper giving the soda giants fits. Coca-Cola accounted for 40.7 percent of U.S. soft drink volume, Pepsi, 31 percent. Coke was trying to introduce a new product to counter gains by Dr. Pepper.

Despite the flattening sales, the profit picture for the industry was bright because of a decrease in the price of sweeteners. "There are a lot of factors to learn about," Harry reflected.

Under the heading "New Directions in the 1990s," Harry discovered that both Coke and Pepsi were increasing their efforts to market noncola brands. Also interesting was the launching of joint ventures with noncola companies, such as one between Coke and Nestle's. "It's not the same soda world my mother knew," Harry observed.

Harry read that U.S. soda companies were aggressively pursuing foreign markets to offset the slowdown in the U.S. market. "The down-home product has an international profit," Harry said with a smile.

In his "For future reference" cards, Harry noted that *Beverage Industry* magazine was cited as a source for much of the article's data. That periodical might come in handy later, Harry knew.

• •

What has Harry gained?

Through careful reading of one reference, Harry has learned:

- That the industry he is researching has several different subsets.
- About the state of the industry's growth (flat).
- That foreign markets were being actively pursued.
- The name of an important trade periodical (*Beverage Industry*).

By devoting an hour to this research, Harry is already far more knowledgeable about the basics of his subjects.

• •

Harry is a thorough person and he wanted to have more than one perspective on an industry where he might consider starting his career. Checking in the reference catalogue again, he came to this citation:

U.S. Industrial Outlook
U.S. Department of Commerce

"I wonder if this volume will provide me with anything new or different," Harry said to himself.

A new age in soft drinks?

Harry surveyed the kind of information he could find in *U.S. Industrial Outlook*. There were about 40 industries discussed, and most had numerous subsets. For example, there was a long section called "Food & Beverage (Overview)." This section included a few pages called "Bottled and Canned Soft Drinks." That was Harry's immediate area of interest, so he turned to that section.

The very first sentence caught Harry's eye. "An unusually cool and rainier summer season dampened U.S. soft drink bottlers' sales in 1992." Harry realized that it is not only farmers who are affected by the weather. Harry noted some other facts, for example:

"The value of exports rose 29 percent. Still, exports account for only 1 percent of industry shipments."

Harry thought for a moment. Considering what he had learned from the *Standard & Poor's Industry Surveys*, this seemed a bit strange. Weren't Coke and Pepsi making a disproportionate amount of profit overseas? Reading further, Harry realized that there is a difference between exports and international sales. Exports must be shipped from the U.S., and overseas sales included drinks produced overseas by a U.S.-owned company. Harry drew a lesson from this experience:

A rule of job search research

Think about what you read and make sure you understand the information you are collecting. Try to identify reasons behind apparent differences in information.

Another aspect of trade called Harry's attention to an important category within soft drinks—unsweetened bottled waters. The U.S. market in this product is dominated by imports, Harry read. "If I were interested in working for a foreign-owned firm in the U.S., this could be an important fact," Harry said to himself.

On the domestic side, Harry noted that colas account for about 70 percent of soft drink consumption "because of their dominance of the more limited selection in the fast-food market." But colas were under pressure in large food stores from "new age" drinks. Further, the name brands were "under attack" from private label colas. Cola giants Pepsi and Coke were introducing their own new age drinks in response.

"It seems that channels of distribution are a major element in selling the product," Harry reflected, "and stores themselves can become competitors. There's more to this industry than taste and labels."

There was a heading for "Long-Term Prospects." "I ought to know which way the experts think this industry is going," Harry thought to himself. He read the opening sentence: "The long-term prospects for the bottled and canned soft drink industry are somewhat cloudy...." The possibility of a change in marketing and distribution strategies was noted. In addition, a possible squeeze on small new age firms by Pepsi and Coke was indicated. "This industry seems to be facing external challenges and intense competition," Harry reflected.

The two reference volumes had given Harry an eye-opening survey of the non-alcoholic beverage industry. But Harry knew that to keep abreast of more recent developments, he should check out the trade journals. He had previously noted that *Beverage Industry* magazine was a source of information, so he decided to go to the library's periodicals room.

· ·

Was the second reference useful?

By utilizing a second reference, Harry has added to his understanding of the industry he is investigating:

• The difference between exports and overseas sales.

• A new subset of the beverage industry (new age drinks).

• The importance of channels of distribution to the industry.

Harry's understanding is now deeper and includes more factors. Both breadth and depth will be important when Harry uses this research to gain job interviews and offers.

· ·

The benefits of periodicals

Harry picked up a current issue of *Beverage Industry* and looked through the articles. He wanted to know what people in the industry had on their minds. Harry noted that there were a variety of short articles.

• "Burger King restaurants serving patrons cappuccino and espresso in Washington State."

• "Gatorade teams with Foot Locker stores in billion-dollar summer promotion."

• "New technology will soon make paperless warehousing a reality."

• "...it takes 6.8 seconds to process a coupon...a more realistic handling fee would be 7 cents instead of 8 cents."

"This industry is about mega-issues like brands and partnerships, but it's also about warehouses and coupons," Harry summarized for himself. There was also a large article about the top 25 firms in the industry. Harry noticed two things immediately. First, the companies were ranked by "gallonage." "Sounds like an important industry term to me," Harry remarked. Second, the top-25 list gave him the major soft drink producers, their gallonage, growth and major products in one handy chart. "This chart gives me material for my cover letters and the beginnings of an outreach list all on one page," Harry realized. Other charts ranked firms by growth and by market share. "I'm learning a lot about an industry and a little about specific firms in one shot," he said with glee.

Harry's joy was increased when his search through the periodicals index under "beverage" identified another magazine, *Beverage World*. Looking through a few issues, Harry found more items of interest. "If I am invited to an interview, I can look at these articles in more detail," Harry reasoned. "At this point, I'll check out items of more general interest." There were plenty of these. For example, Harry found charts on per-capita gallonage consumption, retail receipts (in billions of dollars) and geographic breakdowns on consumption. In addition, Harry noted what he had seen in other sources: Growth in soft drinks had been slow in recent years, about 1.5 percent.

Armed with some basic information about the beverage industry, Harry considered his next step. He wanted to discover what the current issues in the industry were. So Harry decided to use the Info Trac system, which is frequently updated. This friendly computer program in the reference area of his library carried several extensive databases. (Your local or college library probably has Info Trac or similar systems, too). Harry reasoned that the best database for his purposes would be Info Trac's National Newspaper Index. "There should be something in there about beverages," said Harry hopefully.

More than just something! There were 400 news stories listed in the database. Harry quickly realized that his task in this case would be selectivity. "I can't pursue everything. That would take a lot of time and just overwhelm me with data. Let me see what kind of articles could be helpful to me."

Harry quickly decided that references to executive changes and quarterly earnings at various firms were not immediately helpful to him. But a number of other themes seemed to suggest themselves as Harry scanned the list: plans for the future, including new products; competition; foreign markets. Even then, there were more than 150 articles referenced. Harry realized that some current knowledge was what he needed for his cover letters. He would do more extensive preparation if (hopefully, when) he secured an interview. In that light, Harry calculated that five, maximum 10, good articles would be all he needed. Some of the articles Harry decided to read were "A Mexican War Heats Up for Cola Giants"; "One Calorie, Sugar Free, More Cola Flavor"; and "Coke's Creative Ad Strategy."

• •

By reading both a trade publication and the general press, Harry has:

• Identified and ranked the firms in the industry.

• Become aware of current issues in the industry.

• Learned some important terminology.

The ranking will help him develop a mailing list and all three points could improve his cover letters and/or interviews.

• •

Harry had done an excellent job of gathering research for his cover letters, but his job was not done. To be useful, the information had to be organized for easy access. After contemplating several alternatives, this is what Harry decided to do: He reviewed his notes and thought about what would be important to know about an industry. He identified these categories and set up a chart like the one below.

In about two hours, Harry had gathered and organized a significant amount of information on a significant industry. He could use that information in writing to any firm in the beverage industry. Similarly, you could do research on an industry (or nonprofit sector) of interest to you, following the steps that Harry took.

Industry: nonalcoholic beverages

Category of information	Related facts
Major Product Types	Sodas: Includes colas and other sodas, unsweetened bottled waters.
Recent Growth	About 1.5%; soda flattening due to lifestyle changes.
Market Players	Coca-Cola and Pepsi Cola giants in soda — Dr. Pepper giving them fits. (Also: the charts from *Beverage Industry; Beverage World.*)
Profit	Better than growth due to decrease in sweetener cost; international profits per unit higher than domestic (distinction between exports and foreign sales).
Recent News	(I'll fill in this part from daily reading of newspapers.)
Future Trends	Coke and Pepsi moving more into noncolas, especially new age drinks. May force rethinking in marketing and distribution.
Business Issues	Distribution: Burger King serving cappuccino/espresso
Special Terms	Gallonage: Gallons of beverage purchased by consumers
External Influences	Lifestyle, weather, cost of materials, channels of distribution

A fortunate firm

Lauren was handling the project of researching a specific firm. Knowing that the Job Search Club would be handling small firms as an important but separate topic, Lauren decided to investigate a large firm. Lauren was just as "thirsty" as Harry, but she approached research differently than he did. Lauren liked to identify key categories of information before she started her research rather than after. Both approaches have their strong points, Lauren knew, but for her this approach worked best.

Thinking about what she would want to know about a company, Lauren developed the chart on page 32. The left-hand column indicates the categories of information Lauren sought. The middle column summarizes what she found and the right-hand column indicates the source.

Company chart

Name of Company: PepsiCo, Inc.

Category of information		Source of information
Products/ services	• Drinks Note: Specific brand names listed for each product line. • Snack Foods. • Restaurants.	Hoover's
Short history	Invented in 1898. Developed bottling franchises. Ruined by falling price of sugar. Purchased by Loft Candy in 1931. Introduced first radio jingle in 1939. "Pepsi Co." name in 1965, after purchase of Frito Lay.	Hoover's
	1992: Partnership with T.J. Lipton and Ocean Spray.	Annual report
Macro data	Soft drinks sold in 150 countries. Operates more than 6,000 restaurants in U.S.; 1,200 abroad. More than $25billion in sales, 1989; snack food, lowest sales but highest operating income.	Hoover's
Growth	16.6% over past five years.	Annual report
Challenges	Keeping up with changing consumer tactics.	Annual report
Competitors	Nine listed, including: Coca-Cola, McDonalds, Borden & alcoholic content products.	Hoover's
State of industry	Soft drinks experiencing slow growth and intense competition; snack foods and restaurants growing faster.	Hoover's
Management philosophy/ corporate culture	Flexibility; authority & responsibility decentralized.	Annual report
Recent news		Info Trac
Important terms	Flexibility; new age drinks.	

Following a sound research principle, "Start with a general reference before getting deeply involved in specifics," Lauren identified this resource:

Hoover's Handbook:
Profiles of 500 Major
Corporations
The Reference Press, Inc.

This succinct reference addressed many of the things Lauren wanted to know in only one page per firm. Lauren entered the information she gleaned in these categories on her company chart: Products/Services, Short History, Macro Data and Competitors.

The horse's mouth

Lauren realized by looking at her chart that she still needed to learn more about PepsiCo. "Why don't I get some insights straight from the horse's mouth?" she said to herself. Lauren simply called PepsiCo headquarters and asked for the most current PepsiCo annual report. When it arrived about a week later, she started to read through it. "The firm's annual report is a good source because it presents what the firm wants people to think about it, in addition to data required by the government," Lauren thought to herself.

The inside front page provided a summary of financial highlights. Lauren noticed that sales were up compared to the previous year in all three major PepsiCo categories (beverages, snack foods, restaurants) and so was overall income (profit). She saw that restaurant sales were $600 million greater than beverage sales, and that snack food sales were growing faster than the other two categories. "I've got to stop thinking of PepsiCo as just soda," Lauren reminded herself. "This annual report is giving me a more accurate understanding of the firm's products."

On the next few pages, Lauren saw a message from the firm's chairman of the board. In that short space, the chairman focused on flexibility as a central part of the firm's management philosophy. "Local managers have a remarkable amount of authority and power—because they're the ones closest to our customers," the chairman wrote. Lauren realized that if the chairman thought flexibility was central, then she had better understand what it meant at PepsiCo.

The chairman then reviewed the year that had passed by noting that PepsiCo had "continued to reshape our core businesses, dancing to the ever-changing tune of the marketplace."

The chairman summarized a major change in corporate strategy—namely, an effort at global expansion to growing markets, rather than relying on the relative safety of the U.S. business environment. Lauren made note of this change and then reviewed what she had learned for herself: PepsiCo is experiencing growth in each of its three lines of business, with sales at $22 billion. An important component for future growth would be foreign sales. Changing consumer tastes and expanding markets were associated with the central management philosophy of flexibility. Lauren added this information to her chart and continued reading.

The chairman related that as customers changed and wanted more variety, PepsiCo added new products as a means of selling more packages of soft drinks. For example, the firm added the new age category of drinks—those containing only natural ingredients and without preservatives. Lauren had heard of new age drinks before, but she realized she should have a clear understanding of what the term means, not just what it tastes like. Lauren's taste buds received another tingle. The annual report noted that PepsiCo had entered into partnership with T.J. Lipton and Ocean Spray. "One more element of change," Lauren said to herself. "Growth through partnership. Along with new products and overseas markets—that is plenty of change for a flexible management. When I finish my research, I've got to think about what all this would mean to my job search."

Lauren continued reading the PepsiCo annual report and saw that the snack foods and restaurant divisions were also changing as they grew. She took notes on this as well.

••

Annual report as an asset

In the hour or so Lauren spent reading a company's annual report (in this case PepsiCo), this is what she learned:

- Financial highlights.
- "Flexibility" as a company philosophy.
- Reshaping the core market.
- New markets.
- New products.

This information would help Lauren write more persuasively about the talents she could offer the firm and her motivation for joining it.

••

A pressing matter

Even though annual reports tend to be more current than reference books, they are less current (and perhaps less objective) than the print media (magazines, newspapers). Just as Harry had used Info Trac to identify news articles about an industry, Lauren used Info Trac to find current news about a particular company, in this case PepsiCo. She found more than 350 articles in one database (National Newspaper Index) alone! Obviously, Lauren needed to be selective. She identified about a dozen substantive articles, printed out the information summary for later use and entered a few items on her chart.

As a result of this research, Lauren had acquired a reasonably thorough picture of PepsiCo. She could use some of that information to write a cover letter showing that she was sincerely interested in PepsiCo and demonstrating enough of a connection between the firm and herself to be a plausible candidate. If she does obtain an interview, her research will help her interview better. In addition, some of what Lauren learned about PepsiCo would be useful background for other firms marketing beverages as well. This research had taken about two hours.

Would it be necessary to do as much research as Lauren did about a specific company? Not necessarily. But it is better to have material you won't use than to lose the benefits of material you didn't find at all.

Computer research

"I am fairly comfortable using a computer and I am hooked up to the World Wide Web from my personal computer at home. I'll try to do job search research using my computer," Lauren volunteered.

Lauren decided to try researching a profession and a firm from her computer desk at home. "The Job Search Club researched PepsiCo," she said. "Let me see what I can get without leaving my favorite chair."

After connecting to the Web, Lauren entered the home page address (known technically as an URL) for PepsiCo. In this case the address is http://www.pepsico.com. Lauren surmised this would be the address based on her familiarity with other Web addresses.

PepsiCo's home page welcomed Lauren with a picture of a thirsty young consumer and an array of logos for the firm's other divisions. "That would tell me that PepsiCo is more than Pepsi if I didn't already know it," Lauren thought. A menu presented Lauren with a chance to read PepsiCo's mission statement, gain a corporate overview, learn about the PepsiCo Foundation, PepsiCo's environmental commitment and a vehicle to request documents. Lauren clicked on the "environmental commitment." It contained about a dozen pages of text when Lauren printed it out. "Having a good environmental record in the public's eye seems very important to PepsiCo," Lauren concluded. "What's important to the firm is important to the interview," she added pragmatically.

By clicking on clearly labeled icons, Lauren also accessed financial and shareholder information. "The important thing here is to realize that this is the most current data I could probably access," Lauren realized.

The PepsiCo home page also had sections for news from its three large groupings— beverage, snack and restaurant. Because the JSC exercise had focused on beverages, Lauren clicked "beverage news." A menu of recent news stories was at Lauren's fingertips. Some were dated within two weeks of her visit to the Web site.

What Lauren uncovered so far was a wealth of current information that PepsiCo wanted people to know. Was it a substitute for other research? "It's important to know what else is being said about PepsiCo," Lauren realized. "Otherwise, I'll only know what the firm says about itself."

Like many personal computers hooked to the web, Lauren's had several search engines to look for specific topics. She chose one engine, in this case, Magellan, and requested a search for PepsiCo. Several articles were referenced in response. One was a link to information about the firm produced by the publishers of *Hoover's Handbook of American Business.* The material Lauren read was similar to what she would have gotten from the latest volume of the book in the reference library.

Lauren printed out the data and clicked to return to the "menu" page. She saw an item called "similar pages" and clicked on it. On her screen appeared a new page with hypertext links to different web pages referenced. Several were sponsored by a group advocating a boycott of Pepsi in connection with events in South Asia. Another item referred to an article about PepsiCo's efforts to build a presence in Poland. "That's something I probably would have missed in the general press," Lauren mused.

In the course of an hour or so, Lauren found plenty of information about PepsiCo, in its own words and in the views of others. She had sufficient information to complete a helpful company chart like the one illustrated earlier in this chapter.

Researching a field

After Lauren told the Job Search Club how she researched PepsiCo using her personal computer, Harry volunteered to research the beverage industry using the computer in his local library. "I don't have my own computer at home yet, but my local library has several available for public use," Harry said.

Like Lauren, Harry decided to start his search using Magellan as his search engine. "I could start with another engine such as Yahoo or Infoseek just as well," Harry realized. Harry entered the word "beverages" in the box marked "look for" and clicked on the word "search." On the computer screen Harry saw homepages for a variety of beverages including fruit juices, cider, tea and water. In addition, there was a homepage for Coca-Cola, one of PepsiCo's main competitors. "One thing I will learn about beverages will be the variety of liquid refreshments that are competitors in this industry," Harry reasoned. Among the colas, Harry found a homepage for a product that proclaimed the virtues of having twice the caffeine as the industry leaders, and another brand that boasted that it had no caffeine at all. Reading further Harry realized that these brands were fighting for a market share in another part of the country. "That's an important point to note," Harry realized. "There are regional competitors in addition to national ones.

Harry clicked to a page called "food and beverage on the Net" and found that he was now linked to the Yahoo search engine. Harry realized that starting with one search engine didn't preclude easy access to another.

Rather than detailing everything he found, Harry summarized his experience for the Job Search Club. "I compared what I learned from reference books to what I learned from the Web," Harry began. Here are some of his findings:

- There is a wealth of information available about beverages on the Web. It ranges from promotional material to detailed financial statements from the larger companies.
- The information I found on the computer was easier to access and perhaps more diverse than what I found in books. On the other hand, it was less in-depth than a text like *U.S. Industrial Outlook*.
- Having a lot of information is useful only if you think about its significance.

Where are we now?

In this chapter, we followed three members of the Job Search Club as they researched a career, an industry and a firm. We saw the resources they utilized, including commonly available reference books, trade journals, an annual report and a computer base of recent newspaper articles. We also saw how the JSC members organized the information they obtained and how they reflected on the material they were gathering. Altogether, the three parts of this research took between six and 10 hours. You can follow the same steps to research each career, industry or firm of interest to you.

In the next four chapters, we will see how members of the JSC began to draw on their research to write an effective cover letter.

Chapter 3

....

An Opening That Gets Attention

....

In this chapter, the Job Search Club will discuss some basic cover letter issues and then get down to the work of writing an opening paragraph. In the several chapters that follow, we will take an in-depth look at the other three paragraphs of your cover letter.

Thinking about organization and format

Jeannette: Can you give us an organizing principle for writing our cover letters?

Richard: Your cover letter will comprise four main paragraphs:

1. Opening.
   (Why I am writing.)
2. Positive Characteristics.
   (Why you should give me an interview.)
3. Motivation.
   (Why I want to work for you.)
4. Closing.
   (Next step. Keep the ball in your court.)

We will go over each of these four paragraphs in detail before we put together an entire letter. Then we will see how to use a basic letter as a prototype that can be used, with some changes, to write to a large number of employers.

Anthony: Before we go further with the four paragraphs, can you tell us about the proper format for a business letter?

Richard: Three formats are generally acceptable: full block, block and modified block. (These formats are shown on the next few pages.)

Full block format

Your address
City, State, Zip

Date

Name, Title
Company   (Address of person getting your letter)
Street
City, State, Zip

Dear (Mr.; Ms.; Dr.) _____

Opening paragraph   (Paragraphs start at the margin)

Paragraph 2

Paragraph 3

Closing paragraph

Sincerely yours,

                           (Leave room for your signature)

Your name typed

Enclosure

Block format

Your address
City, State, Zip

Date

Name
Title
Company   (Address of person receiving your letter)
Street
City, State, Zip

Dear (Mr.; Ms.; Dr.) _____

Opening paragraph   (Paragraphs start at the margin)

Paragraph 2

Paragraph 3

Closing paragraph

                              Sincerely yours,

                              (Leave room for your signature)

                              Your name typed

Enclosure

Modified block format

This format is like block format except the first line of each paragraph is indented.

Your address
City, State, Zip

Date

Name
Title
Company   (Address of person receiving your letter)
Street
City, State, Zip

Dear (Mr.; Ms.; Dr.) _____

    Opening paragraph

    Paragraph 2

    Paragraph 3

    Closing paragraph

Sincerely yours,

(Leave room for your signature)

Your name typed

Enclosure

In addition to organization and format, the Job Search Club members wanted to discuss principles for determining what should be included or excluded in a cover letter. While there can always be an exception, the guidelines we discussed are generally applicable.

Interest in the next job, not flight from the current one

Harry: How will my letter explain why I am looking for a new job?

Richard: The litmus test for determining what to include or exclude is "Is it likely to help me?" As long as everything you do say is honest, you don't have to say everything.

In terms of your reason for seeking a job: Make your attraction to the next employer very clear. On the other hand, don't explain why you want to leave your current employer, at least not in the first paragraph. The reader's attention should be drawn to where you want to go next, and why. Raising the issue of why you want to leave your current job introduces a negative tone to your letter that could raise a barrier to getting an interview.

Cecily: Would that still be true if you had to find a new job because of a corporate downsizing?

Richard: Some people do mention being caught in a downsizing hoping to make it clear that their loss of employment doesn't reflect on their individual work performance. However, I recommend against it. Usually it is not in your interest to draw attention to being out of work. You may be raising doubts instead of answering them. For example, in a typical downsizing, some people at the firm lose their jobs, most do not. Why is it that you were in the wrong group?

On balance, I would be leery of a statement such as "Due to a recent downsizing at my current employer, I am reentering the job market." While addressing anticipated doubts and reservations can be useful in many circumstances, the safest approach in this case is to stress your connection to the potential new employer. Leave any discussion of downsizing for a face-to-face meeting.

Gabrielle: Your advice to Harry makes sense. After all, he is currently working and that in itself is an attraction to employers. But I haven't been working outside the home for a number of years.

Richard: Your situation is different from Harry's, but let's think this through. The basic principles remain the same. You have positive characteristics that the employer needs in his/her firm. You will also articulate solid reasons why you want to work for that employer in particular.

But there's a glitch. You haven't worked for a number of years. That fact could raise two problems: currency of your skills and your ability to readjust to the work world. None of these need be fatal to your chances.

Here's how I would handle it. First, I would make a short statement about reentering the work force, probably at the beginning of the third paragraph or in the closing paragraph. That way, you quickly explain the chronological gaps on your resume, but do so after presenting your positive characteristics. You could say something like this:

"Now that the responsibility of raising a young family is behind me, I am eager to make my contributions in the workplace again."

Second, if you can indicate that you have retained a connection to the work world, perhaps through a part-time job, say so. If you haven't been working outside the home at all, state your interest in rejoining the work force in the manner I just suggested. Your absence from the work force may carry some problems, but trying to deal with that in a letter will probably not solve them. On the other hand, when you do secure an interview, you will be able to prove your currency and adaptability face-to-face.

David: What about my case? I have a great reason for leaving my current situation. I am graduating college.

Richard: First, congratulations. Second, the same principles still apply. Write what will help you obtain a job interview. Let's think about it. What is the informational content for the reader when you mention your graduation? It says that you are reasonably intelligent and now ready to work full-time. Those are assets, but they don't merit a lot of emphasis. Mention your graduation (whether recent or forthcoming), but still focus on what you can give your next employer and why you want to work for him or her.

In a case like yours, you might open your letter with a sentence like this:

"I am interested in joining the marketing department of your firm when I graduate from Emeritus College in May."

Salary

Gabrielle: Some people suggest mentioning my salary expectations in the cover letter. What do you think?

Richard: In most cases it would be a mistake. Salary information is unlikely to make you more attractive to an employer and it could pose a barrier to interviewing you. It is best to discuss compensation after a job offer is made, not when you are seeking an interview.

There may be two exceptions. First, in some cases a person absolutely, positively wouldn't even consider a position that compensates him/her below a certain dollar amount. This exception is more likely to apply to a highly compensated professional than to the average job-seeker. Second, in some sales situations, a reference to commissions generated may appeal to an employer.

David: Frankly, I'm willing to start cheap — I need experience!

Richard: Your first mistake is selling yourself short in your own mind. Consider the value of your positive characteristics to your next employer. If you are worth the hiring, you are worth a reasonable salary. Second, stating a salary expectation can have a perverse effect. Your expectation is likely to be either too high or too low, and therefore a negative in the employer's eyes. Even if you are right on the mark, that probably won't have a positive influence on your getting the interview.

Lauren: Help-wanted ads are a source of job leads, even though we emphasize self-initiated outreach. Sometimes those ads ask for a salary expectation or salary history. What do you suggest?

Richard: There may be some inclination to ignore that request because of the perverse effect I mentioned to David. In addition, some ads are really attempts to gather salary data per se rather than bona fide announcements of an opening. Still, I would respond in case the ad is legitimate and some reference to salary is necessary even to be considered for an interview.

The best way to respond to questions about salary is with intelligent imprecision. Use a statement such as, "I anticipate a compensation package that is competitive with the market." If you feel the need to geve a number at all, us an elastic expression such as, "in the mid-$20s," rather than giving a specific salary figure such as $25,000. If the request is for a salary history, respond with an imprecise salary expectation or say "My current base salary is in the $30s," rather than detailing every dollar from every job you ever had.

Disabilities

Bill: I have a friend with a significant physical disability. Should she mention this in her cover letter?

Richard: Professionals who deal with disabled clients often refer to this as the disclosure issue: When, if ever, should you disclose that you have a disability? Remember that you are not ethically required to disclose, so the issue falls under our general principle: "Will it help me get an interview?" On that basis, disclosure in the cover letter serves no apparent purpose. Disclosure prior to an interview would make sense, however, under two circumstances:

1. Avoiding social discomfort. If my disability is readily visible, would I prefer to avoid surprise and possible discomfort on the interviewer's part? If the answer is "yes," make disclosure when arranging an interview time.

2. Arranging special needs. If special accommodations need to be in place, such as an ASL interpreter, the prospective employer needs time to make the appropriate arrangements.

The desirability of including capable workers with disabilities in the work force is recognized by the Americans with Disabilities Act. Consult a lawyer or knowledgeable counselor if you feel your rights might have been infringed.

Your opening paragraph: Identify your purpose

After the JSC covered these basic points, we began our discussion about the opening paragraph. The JSC will evaluate some sample opening paragraphs and identify the best approach to take.

The grabber: a few lines that set the stage

After discussing these initial issues, the Job Search Club was eager to start writing their cover letters. Since this was a new topic, I started our session with a few basic remarks. This is a summary of what I shared with them:

- The first paragraph should make the reader interested in reading the rest of the letter. A good approach is to provide the reader with some key information about you that is important to him/her.
- The first paragraph needs to be brief and to the point.

The members of the JSC then wrote sample opening paragraphs for the group to review. I was interested in seeing a "before and after" of how people would start their cover letter. Gabrielle started off the session with this paragraph:

· ·

An opening that won't work

"I am interested in joining your firm in a professional capacity. Although I have no recent background in business, I am certain that my analytical and communication skills would be an asset to your firm. Of particular interest to me would be a position where good interpersonal skills and problem-solving will be appreciated."

· ·

Based on our usual procedure, the JSC members commented on Gabrielle's paragraph in a polite but to-the-point manner. Gabrielle appreciated this because she wanted help landing a job, not a gratuitous pat on the back.

Harry: I think your opening paragraph needs some work. You should be more clear about your purpose in writing.

Harry is right. Get to the point. In most cases, that means using the first sentence of your first paragraph to let the reader know your objective in contacting him/her.

Gabrielle: But certainly the employer knows why I'm writing—I need a job. Why state the obvious?

Lauren: Of course you want a job, Gabrielle. But what kind of a job, and why that job or employer? People are busy, so it's important to get to the point. Maybe you could say something like this, for example:

"I am interested in joining your firm as a commercial lines underwriter."

Gabrielle: But I'm not sure that's what I want to be.

Lauren: No one is suggesting that you marry the company right now. When you say you have an interest in a job or company, that doesn't mean you can't pursue other interests as well. But if you are writing to a particular company, you are better

off having a particular kind of job in mind. If you haven't taken the trouble to identify a purpose in writing, the reader won't take the trouble to consider your letter
seriously. You and I discussed underwriting once, so I chose that as an example.

Listen to Lauren. You can want many kinds of things. Having three or
five goals is not a problem. Having none or 100 is. When you say you are
interested in a particular kind of job, that's true, even if you have other,
unstated interests as well.

Gabrielle: I see what you're saying. Let's move to my second sentence. Didn't
I score some points here? I let the reader know that I have talent, even if I lack
recent professional experience.

Lauren: The way I read that, you seem to be apologizing. If an apology has any
place at all, it's certainly not in the first paragraph. Maybe you could write about
your motivation, for example:

"My interest in this field results from the knowledge that I could contribute many of the skills I have developed throughout my professional
experience."

That way, you are presenting not one but two positive characteristics: Credible
motivation and work experience. Your reference to work experience is honest. You
don't have to mention in the first paragraph that the experience wasn't recent.

Lauren is right, again. The employer is interested in those strengths that
would help his/her firm. Besides, we all have limitations, so raising that fact
as you open your cover letter states the obvious while missing the point.
What if Gabrielle's previous experience had not been at a professional
level? Then she could honestly say "skills I have developed throughout my
working experience."

Gabrielle: That's an interesting point. You want to elicit the reader's interest
early on, and showing a well-founded motivation is a way to do that. From what
people are saying to me, I can see now how my third sentence is too vague. I need
to show more direction and connect with the reader. Let me rewrite that last sentence like this:

"Your company (or name of company) attracted my special interest
during my research of the insurance industry."

Lauren: Good going, Gabrielle! Your research interests the reader because it
suggests that you are serious and directed in your job search.

Following this discussion, I asked Gabrielle to rewrite her opening paragraph. This is what she wrote:

Gabrielle's revised opening paragraph

"I am interested in joining your firm as an underwriter. My interest in this field has developed as a result of my professional experience and my desire to contribute my skills to the maximum. My particular interest in Happyco stems from my research into leading insurance firms in the Midwest."

Harry: It certainly is short.

Richard: Yes, about three sentences is all you should need.

In the optimum case, these are the points you want to convey to the prospective employer:

- Your purpose in writing (in this case to join the firm as an underwriter).
- What motivates your interest in the field. This might include prior experience.
- What attracted you to write to that particular company.
- That you are serious, as indicated by your research, for example.

Three sentences is plenty for that purpose.

David: Gabrielle's opening seems a bit abrupt. Couldn't you start with something like:

David's suggestion: a potential pitfall

"Good morning. I know you're busy, but the two minutes it takes to read this letter will certainly be worth your while."

Richard: You could start that way, but it would not serve your interests. People are incredibly busy these days and they appreciate your getting to the point. In addition, the approach you are suggesting sounds a little hokey. Generally, you are better off when you stick to the basics.

Gabrielle: I'm not really sure what I want. How can I honestly say that I am "interested in joining your firm as an underwriter" or anything else?

Some advice: Avoid gimmicks. You can have a letter that is refreshing and interesting by sticking to the basics.

Richard: You're raising a good point. It's important to be honest. The reality is that when you say you're interested in something, it doesn't mean you are interested in that field or company *only*. As we said earlier, you might have three or five fields of interest to you and any number of companies. What your letter says to the employer is that his/her firm is *one* of those firms and that the career you mention is *one* of those that interest you.

Gabrielle has raised a common concern. It is important to be honest, but what does honesty mean? Everything you say must be true. At the same time, you don't need to say everything that is on your mind.

Gabrielle: But let's say that I really don't have a clue.

Richard: Then it's back to square one: identifying one or more areas of professional interest. Until you have at least one goal identified, it will be hard to ask for something. The "Help, I need a job!" approach never works.

David: What about my situation? My college major was classics. What should I say? "My studies in Cicero have attracted me to being an underwriter (or anything else)"?

Richard: Remember, there is no one-to-one correspondence between college majors and careers. The question is, how did your interest in a particular field develop? Perhaps it was through exposure to a relative in that profession or a summer job or an encounter with someone at a career fair. If you have the interest, it had its origin somewhere.

Let's think this through, David. Could a classics major really be interested in (and hired for) underwriting? Certainly. The core skills are intellectual curiosity, research ability, communication and interpersonal skills. Having any or all of those positive characteristics is not a function of a particular major.

David: Still, could I honestly say that my interest developed as a result of my academic studies?

Richard: Yes, if it's true. But to clarify the connection, you might say, "My interest in underwriting developed when I identified this as a field where I could apply the skills I gained in college." The fact that you took the trouble to investigate a particular career is a plus. In addition, you may arouse some interest in the link between your college experience and a particular profession. Besides, remember that academic studies is a broader concept than just your major, and college experience encompasses more than just academic work.

David: If the connection between your academic studies and the field you are writing about is clear, would it always pay to state that explicitly?

What's all this about underwriting?

In our example, Gabrielle was applying for a position as an underwriter in the insurance industry. Why did we pick this career?

- There are many interesting careers in the insurance industry—for example, underwriter. However, the image of that industry is so negative that many people simply ignore it. That is shooting yourself in the foot. It is to your advantage to challenge your preconceived images about industries and careers when looking for a job.

- A good underwriter needs to have positive characteristics that can be demonstrated, achieved or learned through many kinds of work experiences or fields of study. For that reason, it is an example of the many possible careers people ignore because "it's not what I have done before," or "it's not what I studied."

- People often don't know what an underwriter is, does or enjoys. It pays to investigate a field you may not have considered before.

- Some people confuse underwriting with undertaking. Ignoring a possibility because you don't understand it can be deadly.

Richard: Yes, if you are a recent graduate. It's one way to show that your interest didn't start just yesterday. For example, if Jeannette, an accounting major, wanted to be an auditor, she could refer to "my academic studies in accounting."

This discussion identifies a good rule of thumb: Make sure you make a statement that is both true and credible about the particular firm and/or career. The range of what would be credible is fairly broad. However, it's better to say nothing than make a statement that lacks honesty or credibility.

Now that we had examined the principles involved, each JSC member wrote several opening paragraphs. Here are a few of them:

Jeanette

"I am interested in joining Specialty Cereals, Inc., as a financial analyst. My interest in this area has developed in the course of my part-time job, as well as my academic studies in accounting. The qualifications I can offer your company are..."

Jeannette is about to graduate from college with an accounting major. She stresses her academic studies in the first paragraph because of the easily identifiable connection between her studies and her career goal. This paragraph could be even stronger if Jeannette indicated an interest in the company to which she is writing the way Gabrielle does in this example:

Gabrielle

"As an experienced professional with excellent quantitative skills, I am interested in becoming a financial analyst at Dollarco. I am attracted to your firm because of the praise you have received in *The Wall Street Journal* and from professionals in the field with whom I have discussed my career plans. Here is what I can contribute to your firm..."

Gabrielle follows a good strategy and shows appropriate self-confidence in this version of her opening paragraph. She mentions her professional experience, a decided asset, but doesn't raise her extended absence from the work force, a possible obstacle. In the same sentence, she draws a connection to her field of interest through a positive characteristic, namely quantitative skills. She lets the reader know that she has researched the firm *(The Wall Street Journal)* and has discussed it with "professionals in the field."

This last point is sometimes helpful because people tend to be curious about what others think of them or their employer. Gabrielle's seriousness (research) and tweaking of curiosity provide an inducement to read the rest of her letter.

David

"Kenneth Hart, chief financial officer at Sunderland Savings Bank, suggested that I write to you regarding a position as a market research analyst at Carbo Soda Company. Mr. Hart made this suggestion because he knows of my longstanding interest in market research and my exploration of careers in the beverage industry."

This opening assumes that the person you are writing to knows Kenneth Hart and would react positively to his name. (Finding the Kenneth Harts in your life is the subject of Chapter 11.) David used the technique of a third-party testimonial in the second sentence. Since the reader knows Kenneth Hart, the statement about David's longstanding interest gains more credibility.

Lauren

"I am interested in joining your staff in a policy analyst role. My interest in Blubber Is Our Brother stems from a desire to contribute my talent to a cause that has aroused my passion: saving the whales. Let me tell you what I can contribute to the goals of your organization."

Lauren is using good sense here. When applying to a nonprofit or advocacy group, it's important to remember that these are professional organizations with a serious purpose.

Therefore, you need to make it clear that you are a serious person who can make serious contributions. Passion for the cause by itself won't get you the interview, let

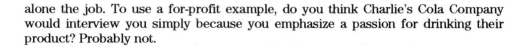

alone the job. To use a for-profit example, do you think Charlie's Cola Company would interview you simply because you emphasize a passion for drinking their product? Probably not.

Bill

"As a forthcoming graduate in industrial engineering, I am interested in joining Manufacturing Designs. My interest in your firm was sparked during a series of projects I completed as part of my engineering training. I know you need people of exceptional talent, so let me tell you why you should consider me for an interview..."

In this case, Bill, an engineering major in college, is seeking to apply directly the technical training he received in college. For this reason, he is thinking clearly when he indicates his field of study in the first sentence of his opening. Since academic projects in engineering are often closely related to real-world uses, Bill's statement about his projects is credible. In some cases, it would make the opening more powerful to mention the name of your college:

- If your college is very prestigious, especially in your field. Examples would be MIT in engineering or Amherst College in liberal arts.
- If there is some basis for a connection between your college and the firm. This would include geographic proximity, a very prominent alumnus in that firm or a history of hiring a large number of graduating students from your college.

Anthony had been in his profession for about five years and felt it was time to take a career step in the same field. In this letter, Anthony uses a name linking himself to the person addressed in his letter.

Anthony

"I am writing at the suggestion of Tom O'Reilly, your co-chair of the Hampton Beach Civic Forum. Tom suggested I contact you because there may be a match between the talents I have developed as a finance professional and your needs. Let me tell you about some of my achievements with my current employer."

If you have a connection to the person receiving your letter, mention that connection in the first sentence. In this case, Anthony can grab "Mr. Jones's" attention by mentioning the name of a colleague to him. Mr. Jones will probably take some positive step for the sake of his relationship with Tom O'Reilly. If the individual reading the mail works for Mr. Jones, that person will pay special attention to Anthony's letter to protect his or her relationship with Mr. Jones.

In the second sentence, Anthony used good judgment in moving forward to his possible role in Mr. Jones's firm. Don't dwell on your connection or it will appear that you have nothing of your own to offer.

••

Cecily

"I am assessing my next career step and working for your firm in a customer service capacity seems like a perfect choice. Here are some of the characteristics I can contribute to your company."

••

Cecily has been caught in a downsizing, but that is not a statement she should make in her opening paragraph. Instead, she states why she is writing and provides an incentive to read her letter. Cecily has done this by indicating an interest in taking the next step in a specific career—customer service.

Harry had a job, but he wanted to move to another profession. This is the opening paragraph that Harry wrote:

••

Harry

"I am a successful small businessman with extensive ties in this community. At this point in my career, I am interested in utilizing my business sense, interpersonal skills and persuasive ability to become a stockbroker. I am certain that I could be a successful producer for Alan Green & Sons."

••

Harry presents the reader with two good reasons to take him seriously in the very first sentence (businessman; community ties). Then Harry specifies three characteristics that would make him an asset. The third sentence serves as a transition to the next paragraph.

There is no reason for Harry to mention his current job (store manager) or why he wants to leave his present situation. That information would serve only to lessen the incentive to read the rest of Harry's letter.

Some variety

The examples developed by the Job Search Club give us a good understanding of writing an opening paragraph that grabs the reader's attention. Let's take a look at some additional examples:

Part-time work. "As a local resident with proven computer skills, I am seeking a part-time position in your data processing department. Several of my neighbors work for your firm and have mentioned how work loads have increased recently. Perhaps my skills could help meet your current needs."

Recent news. "The article in the *Local Ledger* about Plushco Toys caught my attention. I noticed that you are developing a new line that is especially squeezable. My years of experience in soft material design may provide a good source of talent in those efforts."

"Your observations about the significance of employee morale, quoted on WCPN News, struck a chord with me. I, too, have been keenly aware of how intangibles such as morale affect the bottom line. I would like to meet with you to explore the possibility that my experience could be of benefit to your firm."

••••••••••••

New geography. "I have been exploring growth firms like yours in the Seattle area because I will be settling there in the near future. My research indicates that Sonicboom, Inc., may be just the firm to utilize my experience in rapid-flight noise makers."

"I am interested in joining your firm's marketing department, particularly in a research capacity. My current employer also makes high-end impulse items, so Yourco naturally came to mind as I planned my forthcoming move to San Antonio."

Similar functions, new industry. "We met a few years ago at a technical writer's conference in Albany. I have recently been looking for possibilities for applying my skills in a growth industry, an area in which Fertilawnco is a shining example. I wonder if we can meet to discuss opportunities for me to contribute to Fertilawnco."

Similar industry, new function. "You and I share a professional history in the widget industry. Over the last year or so, I have been exploring the next step I want to take. I am convinced that the best way to apply my talents and interests is to pursue a position in the production and distribution of widgets. In that connection, I would appreciate meeting with you personally."

Where are we now?

In this chapter, the Job Search Club learned how to write an opening paragraph that attracts the reader's interest by addressing the reader's professional needs in a succinct manner. We identified six helpful ideas for a good opening paragraph and the JSC members wrote a number of examples. We checked to make sure that each paragraph achieved at least these goals: elicited reader interest by explaining your purpose in writing; stated what motivates your interest; demonstrated your seriousness; and achieved brevity. In the next chapter, we will look at how your second paragraph tells the employer, "This is why you should interview me."

Chapter 4

••

Why You Should Interview Me

••

In this chapter, we will learn how the Job Search Club members identified those positive characteristics to highlight in the second paragraph of their cover letter—the paragraph dealing with "why you should interview me." We will also learn how to connect your past to your future, use convincing examples to validate your statements and match the positive characteristics you have to the qualities an employer needs.

Why it's better to give than to receive

The next meeting of the Job Search Club had an air of excitement mixed with concern. On the one hand, we were rolling. The JSC members had a good grip on the why and how of an opening paragraph. On the other hand, there was some concern about our new topic, the second paragraph. Putting ourselves on the line by identifying characteristics we think address an employer's needs can be a little frightening. To dispel some of the anxiety, we opened up with questions.

Gabrielle: What is the rationale for structuring the second paragraph as you suggest: telling the firm what you can do for them?

Richard: There are three main reasons. First, it's better to give than to receive. This is a good business practice, not just a popular saying. Remember, looking for a good job requires business sense. Tell the reader what you can do for him or her and you will sustain interest by addressing his or her needs. At some level, most people want to know "what's in it for me" before investing time, energy and attention.

Second, it's rarely obvious what you can do for the employer. Even if you have been working for a number of years, your positive characteristics need to be made explicit. Don't depend on the employer to make assumptions in your favor. If you are just leaving school or returning to the work force, identifying what you have to offer is especially important, because it won't be clear from the context of your current experience.

Third, you want to allay skepticism. If you are a recent college graduate, there is a suspicion that you don't know what you want professionally and believe that the world owes you a living. An experienced worker needs to show that he or she is thinking in terms of the next employer's needs rather than expecting to reenact his

••••••••••••

53

or her glorious experiences with the last one. Remove this type of skepticism about you by identifying what you can give before explaining what you can get.

History as my witness

Cecily: When we say we have certain positive characteristics, why should anyone believe us?

Richard: Good question. You can establish credibility by giving good examples of how you demonstrated, achieved or learned characteristics. Remember, you want to give the employer sufficient reason to interview you. At the interview, the firm will probe your characteristics in greater depth. A related point: As the following story illustrates, your past behavior is used as a predictor of your future behavior.

••

The historical factor: your past as predictor

The value of the past to the job search is that it is a useful predictor about your future. It's true that where we are today is not exactly where we were yesterday or two years ago. Still, the stream of your life tends to flow in some general direction and contain some general characteristics (fast-moving or just a trickle, broad or very narrow, holds up in a drought or just dries up). Although your daily activities may change from year to year, who you are does not change dramatically once you have become an adult.

To apply the historical factor: If you show an employer that you were a creative, energetic person with good organizational skills in the past, s/he can predict with a reasonable degree of accuracy that you will be a creative, energetic person with good organizational skills in the future.

••

Bill: Even so, how do we know what it is that you want to give a particular employer? You have emphasized that each of us has many positive characteristics. This is a cover letter, not an autobiography. How do we know which of our positive characteristics to highlight?

Richard: Here is a good opportunity to utilize some of the research we discussed at an earlier session (see Chapter 2).

Do you remember the research David did about careers? He built an inventory of characteristics important to a particular career, market research in that case, to share with the JSC. Anyone seeking a career in that field can look at the inventory and identify those characteristics that s/he feels best about.

Similarly, we built an inventory of information about a particular industry to show how it could be done for any industry. We can look at the appropriate inventory and identify a match between our positive characteristics and the needs of that industry. Examples would be creativity, ability to deal with change and time management. Very often our research about the particular firm will also identify positive characteristics it needs that we have to offer. Examples would be product knowledge, familiarity with the client base, experience with a similar company or, as Lauren discovered, flexibility.

Let's write a sample second paragraph (why you should interview me) and then we can see how to apply these ideas in practice.

••••••••••••

Gabrielle volunteered to start, using market research as her desired career for the sake of this letter. Her draft utilized a format that is easy to modify when so desired and easy to read as well:

••

Gabrielle's draft,
"why you should interview me" paragraph

"There are a number of skills I can contribute to your firm:

Research. My research and recommendations were utilized by a local advocacy group designing its appeal to the general public.

Analyzing. Analyzed demographic/voting pattern data to determine best approach to specific constituencies.

Presentation. Used self-made graphs and diagrams to make oral presentations in both classroom and other settings.

Computers. Experienced in using computer packages as a research, analytical and graphic-making tool."

••

The JSC members looked over Gabrielle's draft and asked her some questions.

David: Could you tell us why you chose that particular format? Somehow I was expecting a regular paragraph.

Gabrielle: There are several reasons. First, it encourages the reader's eyes to fall on the skills I have to offer. Second, this format makes changes easy, at least in a mechanical sense. Third, it's easier to type than a regular paragraph, although with a word processor that may not be a big issue.

Gabrielle could have added a fourth reason: It may be a better format for computer scanning (see Chapter 7).

Cecily: How did you choose which of your positive characteristics to include?

Gabrielle: The subject of this paragraph is "why you should interview me." I looked at the chart of skills needed in market research. (See Chapter 2.) First, I identified needed skills where I felt the strongest. If I had a strong example to support the skill, I used it. If my examples were weak, I didn't. Then I realized that some of the skills overlap, for example, "Presentations" and "Making Diagrams." In a case like that, I was able to cover both skills with one sentence.

Harry: I understand how you identified the skills you mentioned, but how did you identify the examples you wanted to use?

Gabrielle: I wanted examples from experiences that were as closely related to a professional usage as possible. That's why I wrote about an "advocacy group designing its appeal to the general public," for example.

David: Do you feel your examples are strong?

Gabrielle: My examples are as strong as I can make them. Obviously, if I had worked part-time in market research, let's say as an interviewer or data analyst, I would have a stronger example. But that wasn't the case, so I showed where I did utilize skills the field requires.

David: How did you decide on the order of your positive characteristics?

•••••••••••

Gabrielle: I had two things to keep in mind. First, what would be the most important characteristic in the eyes of the firm? Second, where did I have the strongest example? In this case, research came out first on both counts, since it seems to be the core of the job.

Cecily: We consider ethics to be important in our job search. Do you consider your example for "analyzing" to be honest. You neglected to mention that it took place as part of a civic organization's project.

Gabrielle: Yes, it is honest. Remember our rule: Everything you say in a job search must be true, but you don't have to say everything. I stated that I had utilized a skill, but said nothing about the setting. If the setting is important to the firm, they can decide to seek more details on the resume, not to interview me at all or ask me about it at the interview if there is one.

Bill: I notice that the points you mentioned are all generic to market research as a profession. Are there other points you might raise?

Gabrielle: Yes, when it comes to writing to a specific firm, I might include a statement about product knowledge, client familiarity, experience with firms of a similar size or other connections between what I offer and what they need.

When the JSC members finished their questions to Gabrielle, I asked each of them to draft a "why you should interview me" paragraph of their own.

Harry was considering changing fields and had to think about showing the usefulness of his current profession, supermarket manager, to a new one. For the sake of this exercise, Harry decided to write to a freight forwarder. Drawing from his research on freight forwarding, Harry identified positive characteristics he had demonstrated, achieved or learned in his current career that would be useful in his next field. Harry's paragraph appears below.

The JSC members wanted to ask Harry a few questions.

Jeannette: What purpose does your first sentence serve? It doesn't seem to give any particular reason to interview you.

Harry's draft, second paragraph

"I am certain I can make a substantial contribution to your firm, just as I have for my current employer. For example, I have shown myself to be a highly organized professional who can juggle many projects simultaneously without succumbing to fatigue or stress. The large volume of products I deal with requires a knowledge of interstate shipping procedure and the ability to schedule shipments effectively. In a highly competitive market, I have been able to establish pricing that yields a fair profit without losing customers."

Harry: I had two reasons. First, I wanted a sentence to transition between paragraphs. Second, I wanted to make it clear that I am currently employed. Unfortunately, there is some skepticism about people who don't have a job, so I wanted to remove that skepticism as it might relate to me.

David: How did you pick the positive characteristics you presented?

Harry: I am switching fields, so it is especially important to show positive characteristics that are important in both my current and anticipated fields. My research identified several characteristics needed by freight forwarders that I have certainly demonstrated or learned in the retail field.

Cecily: Is there any particular reason for the order of your sentences?

Harry: Letter-writing isn't an exact science, but I tried to put first the characteristic that would appeal most. In freight forwarding, the well-organized, tireless employee is a real asset, and I have demonstrated those characteristics in the past. The sentences about inventory and pricing suggest I have some exposure to two pragmatic parts of the business.

Cecily: The shipments you deal with now are mostly incoming. The freight forwarder arranges a lot of sending. Is this a good example?

Harry: It is certainly honest. My statement doesn't claim experience with outgoing shipping. The example should still be helpful to me because it deals with shipping, a function common to both my current and future careers.

Let me share with you "why you should interview me" paragraphs from other JSC members and my comments about them.

••

Bill
(a graduating industrial engineering student)

"In the course of my engineering program, I have mastered mathematics, science and computer skills, in addition to engineering principles. Many of our class assignments were group projects from which I learned how to apply principles to practice. For example, my project on 'Nuts and Bolts Meets Flesh and Blood' addressed a key production problem in your industry. Through my leadership role in student government, I enhanced my communication and interpersonal skills."

••

Bill is demonstrating a good grasp of what he needs to show a prospective employer. In the case of a highly technical profession, it is a good idea to establish your technical ability early in the letter. It is also helpful to show how you have used your technical training in practice. Since Bill didn't have directly applicable work experience, he cited his class projects. True, applicable work experience would be the most powerful attraction. However, if you can't honestly refer to the most attractive experience, cite the most compelling you can offer. Notice how Bill mentioned group projects. Working well in a team is a major asset in Bill's profession. Similarly, the communication and interpersonal skills Bill cites will be important to his employer.

Bill's paragraph related a class project to the needs of a particular industry. He could make his letter even stronger if he links some of his skills to a specific service of the firm to which he is writing.

....

Cecily
(an experienced worker about to be downsized out of a job)

"I am certain that the talent I have shown throughout my corporate experience would make me an asset to your firm:

Client relations: I respond to client needs, not just to complaints. Clients have praised both the substance and style of what I do for them.

Efficiency: Recognizing that customer service helps keep a business profitable, I trained my staff to respond to customer inquiries quickly and thoroughly.

Product knowledge: I have mastered more than 60 new product introductions with only a few days' lead-time.

Flexibility: I have adapted to the changing work environment resulting from new clients, new products and new management."

....

Cecily needs to show success in her old job and assuage any doubt about her ability to adapt to a new one. By mentioning client relations and efficiency, Cecily has described the essence of her past success. The examples given for product knowledge and flexibility indicate the ability to adapt to new situations.

When writing to a specific employer, Cecily could make her paragraph stronger. She should draw parallels between her past experience and the requirements of a potential employer in areas like customer service, type of clients or product categories.

Four more sample paragraphs

Let's take a look at sample second paragraphs written by other members of the Job Search Club:

....

Lauren
(wants to move from the corporate to the nonprofit sector)

"*The Non-Profit Monthly* recently noted three important criteria for professionals who want to make a difference through a nonprofit career. The first is organization, a skill I have developed with my current and previous employers. The second is commitment to a larger purpose, which my seven years of school board service readily demonstrate. The third is a sensitivity to a variety of external constituents, a talent exhibited through my experience in marketing."

....

Anthony
(wants to advance his current career in finance)

"Because you are a seasoned professional, there is no need for me to tell you what it takes to be a finance manager. Let me tell you, instead, why I am ready to take on that responsibility. Of primary importance is the ability to access the information I need and analyze its implications for my projects. In addition, I have a track record of making timely decisions that incorporate the needs of other functional areas such as marketing and production. While I have not managed a large staff per se, I have demonstrated excellent interpersonal and motivational skills."

....

Jeannette
(a graduating senior with a business major)

"I know that you are looking for people of exceptional ability, so let me tell you about the skills I can bring to Yum-Yum Cereals.

Business experience: gained through two internships, one with a consumer food products company, Delicious Treat.

Analytical ability: developed and honed through business courses.

Leadership ability: demonstrated by my role in student government and my sorority.

Time management: proven by obtaining high grades while working 20 hours a week."

....

David
(a graduating liberal arts major)

"Let me tell you how my education and work experience have given me the tools I need to make a clear contribution to your firm from the very beginning. First, I have shown that I am an innovative doer who can think out of the box. My work as supervisor will readily attest to that. Second, I have a strong work ethic. I self-financed 80 percent of my total college costs through work and loans. Third, I am a team player in class projects, on the job and in intramural sports."

....

Where are we now?

We have seen how the Job Search Club drew on previous research to identify positive characteristics the employer would need. The JSC members learned why the "why you should interview me" paragraph is so important and how to think about what to include in it. You saw different second-paragraph texts with some comments on each.

In the next chapter, we will look at the third paragraph: "why I want to work for you."

Chapter 5

••

Why I Want to Work for You

••

So far, the Job Search Club had gained a good grasp on the first two paragraphs of their cover letter. The third paragraph, "Why I want to work for you," lets you tell the employer why you are seeking a particular kind of job and/or writing to that particular company. A statement showing your attraction to a company indicates that you aren't just fishing about for a job. That in itself will give you an advantage over your competitors. It is especially critical for recent college graduates and people returning to the work force. Their motivation is almost never self-evident from an existing career path and is often suspect in the eyes of employers.

John and Mary: a scene to avoid

Imagine this scene: John would like to invite someone to a dance. He phones Mary, a lovely woman with whom he has never gone out.

John: Mary, I want to invite you to the Barn-burners Dance on Saturday.

Mary: Why are you interested in going with me, John?

John: Heck, I need a date, don't I?

The highest probability is that Mary and John will not be dancing together Saturday night. In both job searches and romantic searches, people tend to want to know what is your particular interest in them.

After a few wry smiles, the JSC members started to discuss the implications of the John-and-Mary story for their cover letters. It is important to identify your motivation as it relates to a particular job for several reasons, the group concluded:

- To show that you have a clear motivation for seeking an interview beyond "Help, I need a job."
- To demonstrate that there is a realistic connection between what you want and what the employment situation provides. If there is, you will be a more attractive interview candidate for the firm.

Harry raised a question: Would we need to think about our motivation afresh with each letter or could we say the same thing to each employer?

••••••••••
61

I explained to Harry that there is an intermediate approach, which is more effective than the extremes he mentioned. You can develop an inventory of what motivates you. Then:

- Write your prototype third paragraph.
- Make changes as necessary drawing on your inventory.

I asked Harry how he would approach those two steps.

Harry thought for a while and rephrased the question to make it more comfortable for his own use: "I need to identify what I want from my next job. I can start by making a list."

Harry's list, which he could change as our letter-writing project developed, contained five things he wanted:

- Compensation.
- Chance to use skills.
- Location.
- Opportunity to advance.
- Pleasant co-workers.

I told Harry that his list would make the start of a good inventory, but it could be taken a step further. At that point Gabrielle suggested an idea. Gabrielle thought about combining her "want list" with what the firm has to offer. This is an important step because indicating your motivation will help only if it matches with what the firm has to offer. Analyzing the situation, Gabrielle saw three areas where a particular employment situation might meet a job-seeker's wants:

- The job itself.
- The industry.
- The firm.

Combining ideas, Harry and Gabrielle were able to design a chart like the one on page 63. In this case, Gabrielle had marketing research for Drinkco in mind. Not everyone was convinced that the I want/the employer offers chart was the way to go. "I would hate to do one of these every time I did a cover letter," Lauren said. "It looks like a lot of work!" Gabrielle put the chart in a more realistic perspective:

"Actually, if you think it through and organize carefully, many elements of the chart will remain constant. First, remember that what you want won't change from employer to employer; only what you're likely to get will change. For any specific kind of profession (like market researcher, accountant, sales representative, writer), what you would expect to get relative to what you want should be reasonably constant. Similarly, the column on 'industry' should remain constant for all firms in a given industry. Only one column will change from case to case—the company."

I want/the employer offers chart (for Drinkco)
Satisfied by:

What I want in next job	Job	Industry	Company
Challenge	beat competitors	new products	fighting giants
Variety		new products	
Money			(compensation?)
Apply skills	research uses		
Location			not great but acceptable
Growth			they have big plans
Other wants that may come to mind			

Jeannette was concerned about the last part: "The motivation for wanting a firm could be difficult to identify without firm-specific research," she objected.

Since David had handled the project on individual research, he entered the discussion: "It would be great to make some specific reference to the firm," David agreed. "But if time doesn't permit the type of research I did on Pepsico, you might be able to utilize information gathered researching the industry." Remember, Harry told us how his industry research also yielded information about specific firms. If that doesn't work, you could make a statement about the appeal of a firm's size or location to you. Let me show you an example.

A generic motivation for wanting a particular firm

"...I am particularly attracted to your firm because I am interested in pursuing my career with a mid-sized service provider in the San Jose area."

David is making a good point here. We organized our research into three categories (careers, industries, companies/firms) for ease of execution. However, life doesn't fit into neat, self-contained categories. Very often, what we learn in one context is useful in another.

There is a second part to David's observation. Sometimes we are operating under constraints such as time or energy, which compel us to do the best we can under the circumstances. In that case, indicate the importance of a generic characteristic that would be applicable to the particular case. Examples would be type of industry, size of firm and geographic area.

Gabrielle wanted to know how many points to make in the third paragraph. Two or three would be about right. Try to identify one motivation linked with each of our three categories (job, firm, industry). However, it is better to say nothing than something that is not true or not believable.

So why do I want to work for you?

The JSC decided it was time to write a "why I want to work for you" paragraph. We decided to use the case of market research for a nonalcoholic beverage company as our example. Gabrielle wrote the following draft, drawing on the research Lauren, Harry and David had gathered:

Gabrielle's draft, "why I want to work for you" paragraph

"My decision to pursue a career in market research flows from my desire to apply my skills to a profession where variety and change can be enjoyed. The beverage industry appeals to me because of its fierce competition for market share and the constant introduction of new products. I read in *Beverage Weekly* that Drinkco is especially intent on challenging the cola giants. A growing firm with big plans is where I want to start my career."

The JSC members looked at Gabrielle's draft and offered their ideas:

Lauren: You gave reasons for wanting to work for Drinkco based on the three components we discussed earlier: the job itself, the firm, the industry. That's definitely a strength.

David: I think there is room for improvement, though. For example, your first sentence says ". . . where variety and change can be enjoyed." It seems that you took the words directly from the Job Chart. Instead of "can be enjoyed" you should say "are a part of the job." That would be more in keeping with the tone of a business letter.

Doing it badly

Luckily, Gabrielle didn't write a paragraph like this one:

"I want to work for Plotco because I seek a challenging work environment in a dynamic, growing industry. My writing skills and drama interests should fit right in with your product line."

Although words such as "dynamic" and "growing" sound good, they are inappropriate to Plotco. In this case, writing and drama skills are also not selling points. It would have been apparent that Gabrielle neglected to find out that Plotco was in fact the sole surviving firm in a shrinking industry that undertakes the tedious work of locating the burial plots of people who died during the McKinley administration.

Gabrielle: I see what you mean. When we draw facts from one of our charts, we may have to amend the wording to find the appropriate tone for our letter. How about the second sentence?

Lauren: I was thinking of David's research. He noted that Pepsico is much more than Pepsi, even more than sodas in general. It's important for us to make sure that we don't incorrectly identify the firm's industry or identify just a part of it when more is involved.

Gabrielle: That is a valid point, Lauren. However, in this case, Drinkco produces only beverages, so the statement "the beverage industry appeals to me" makes sense. If I were writing to Pepsico, I could make reference to my interest in their beverage division. My opening paragraph should specify the beverage division also. On the other hand, if I meant the whole company, I might say "consumer food industry."

Harry: What would you do if a fact that applies to the industry as a whole doesn't apply to Drinkco? For example, what if Drinkco has a product they have been marketing for years with no plans to introduce a new product?

Gabrielle: There are several possibilities. One, I could leave the sentence alone. Competition for market share exists whether a particular firm is a major player or not. For example, somebody is trying to displace Drinkco with a similar soda or an alternative beverage appealing to the same consumers. Second, I could drop the clause about "new products" if that doesn't apply to Drinkco. Third, I could drop the whole sentence if I know that Drinkco is not typical of its industry. Personally, I would go with the second choice since it shows knowledge of the industry without implying something inaccurate.

Harry: Let me push this a little further. What if Drinkco is perfectly happy with its market share and doesn't engage in "fierce competition."

Gabrielle: If they are not competing for market share (or new markets), they don't need a market researcher anyway. I chose to mention "fierce competition" because that's what makes a market researcher so valuable. Still, in the case you mentioned I should consider eliminating the phrase about competition, or at least toning it down.

Gabrielle has made a number of good points in this dialogue:

- Be careful to take information from your inventories that is accurate and relevant to the situation at hand.
- What you know about the firm may affect what you say about your interest in the industry and vice versa.
- Write based on the best knowledge available to you at the time.
- It makes sense to choose a statement about the industry that is particularly relevant to the field you want to enter.

Let me share with you other draft paragraphs and summarize the comments that were made about them:

David's draft on page 66 reads smoothly, but he needs to be careful about the content. If you describe a work environment, make sure you are accurate. If David has a reliable source for referring to "fast-paced" and "creative," it makes sense to use those terms. But don't use words just because they sound good. If the working environment at Sundance is slow and methodical, David's sentence would reveal that he doesn't understand the firm.

David's draft

"I would like to become a member of the Sundance Marketing team because I perform best in fast-paced, creative work environments. Product management appeals to me because I enjoy the challenge of having responsibility for a project from start to finish. In addition, I spent most of my childhood living in Waltham, and I plan to settle in that area."

Product managers generally have a start-to-finish responsibility, so David's expressed interest is right on target. Expressing a credible connection to a firm's geography also makes sense if you are currently living elsewhere. Your childhood is a credible connection. Your favorite baseball team is not.

Jeannette's draft

"A career in financial analysis with Gauger Credit would be very appealing to me. It would enable me to pursue my interest in this field with a company praised by *The Wall Street Journal* as "a shining light in the world of corporate finance." In addition, I wish to work for a medium-sized company since that is an environment I have found conducive to gaining a broad perspective on an entire functional area."

Jeannette focuses on attributes of the company (*The Wall Street Journal*; medium-sized). She has clearly done her research and thought about the significance of the firm's size. Those are big pluses. Jeannette may not care about a firm's product or services as long as she can be in financial analysis. If a particular circumstance doesn't matter, say nothing rather than faking an interest.

Lauren was interested in applying talents developed in the for-profit sector to a nonprofit organization. But in an effort to show her connection to the group's cause, Lauren hurt herself.

In the following paragraph, Lauren forgot to balance her enthusiasm for the cause with a statement of interest in a particular job. She said a lot about whales, but nothing about the organization.

Lauren's ill-advised paragraph

"I have been a long-time devotee of whales. Last summer I went on six whale watches and sponsored a neighborhood showing of *Save Willie*. I am boycotting Norway and have picketed the Hartford Whalers hockey team. As a person who cheered when Captain Ahab got what was coming to him, I'm sure I would finally find a working home with Blubber Is My Brother."

Lauren has shown two potentially negative characteristics, an obsession with a subject and a discomfort with co-workers in the past ("...finally find a working home..."). Lauren reconsidered the matter and redrafted her paragraph:

Lauren's better advised paragraph

"I am interested in pursuing a career with Blubber Is My Brother (BIMB) for several reasons. First, I would like to lend my marketing and communications skills to an organization whose goals I have supported for several years. Second, my discussions with people in the field have convinced me that BIMB is the type of organization that values the contributions of all its staff members. Third, since nonprofit organizations like yours tend to take a long view on issues, I anticipate an environment where employees are encouraged to look beyond the next quarterly report."

Lauren has now stated her interest in whales without letting that fact dominate her paragraph. She has also indicated in her third sentence why she is attracted to a nonprofit organization after years in the corporate sector.

Anthony's draft

"Advertising Associates would be a perfect place for me to continue my career. Your operating motto, 'Facts sell,' describes my approach to presenting a product or service. In addition, I am impressed by the twin characteristics of creativity and integrity that helped you win an Effie Award in 1994. Looking at the future, the fact that you were able to attract the Longhorn Industries account from a much larger competitor shows that Advertising Associates has the potential to be a growing firm even in a difficult market."

Here, Anthony is showing that he has researched the firm thoroughly. He identifies with the firm's culture (such as "Facts sell," creativity and integrity). He also presents his pragmatic side by referring to client acquisition (Longhorn Industries) and potential. This is a good paragraph because Anthony shows a personal and practical interest in the firm.

In the following paragraph, Cecily has identified an attraction to the prospective employer based on three factors: the industry, the firm and the job. By doing this, she has shown a serious interest in the total environment in which she would be working. Cecily's previous experience as a customer service representative was not in the retail industry. Therefore, showing that she has researched the firm and its industry adds significantly to her credibility.

Cecily's draft

"The possibility of continuing my career with Fantastic Stores, Inc., appeals to me for several reasons. The retail industry in general appeals to me because of the creativity needed to keep up with anticipated changes in consumer tastes. Applying my skills in your company would be especially interesting. Your chairman, Mr. John Marvin, announced a commitment to attracting the aging baby boomer market, a group in which I have taken a personal interest. Most of all, I am attracted to the fact that Fantastic Stores expects its customer relations people to be client-base builders, not just a complaint department."

In the following paragraph, Bill is linking his motivation to Manufacturco's approach to operations. Note that he indicates an interest with both history (junior year in college) and continuity (18 months of research; initial attraction to field). This is a far more compelling approach than saying "I have always been interested in working for a firm like yours." This paragraph could be stronger if Bill indicated some knowledge of the general industry (electronics; appliances; textiles).

Bill should consider writing directly to Sally Greene if she still works for Manufacturco. If he does, he would change his first sentence: "Ms. Greene, it was you who first interested me in a career with Manufacturco..." or "I first became interested in Manufacturco when you spoke in my class about..."

Bill's draft

"My attraction to Manufacturco began when I was a junior in college. Ms. Sally Greene, your production supervisor, spoke to our class about ways to meet new efficiency standards in a relatively short period of time. I was impressed by the innovative approaches Manufacturco had introduced, which combined both worker and machine in the process. During the next 18 months, I researched various approaches to efficiency, and discovered that your firm was frequently mentioned as a leader in decreasing costs without downsizing. Working for a company that makes a profit without discarding people is exactly what attracted me to industrial engineering in the first place."

Harry's opening line (following) presents a punchy introduction to the rest of the paragraph. But there is more to the paragraph than an appealing opening. Harry proceeds to explain his interest in the job, firm and industry. Further, Harry shows an understanding of a major event influencing the industry (growth in trade) and a particular attribute of the firm to which he is writing (expanding client base).

Harry's draft

"Working for Foremost Brothers appeals to me because it would be the right job in a great firm in a growing industry. Being a freight forwarder combines the talents I enjoy utilizing the most: organization, communication and business sense. With international trade expanding, the freight forwarding industry should have new opportunities for growth. In that context, your firm is especially attractive to me becase you have shown an ability to expand beyond a traditional group of clients."

Most freight forwarders are relatively small concerns. If Harry decided to pursue this field, he would probably want to read Chapter 12 to learn how to find information on small businesses.

Where are we now?

In this chapter, the Job Search Club members learned how to write a third paragraph ("Why I want to work for you") that provides two or three credible connections between what you want and what working for a particular firm offers.

Harry and Gabrielle designed a chart that will help you organize an inventory of ideas you can use for your third paragraph. It is based on qualities you want that you hope to find through the job you are seeking, the firm and the industry of which it is a part. This type of chart can be used as a resource in writing the third paragraph of your cover letter.

By listening in to JSC discussions, you learned how to review each sentence in your paragraph to make sure it conveys appropriately the message you want to send.

In the next chapter, we will see how to write a short closing paragraph that leaves the initiative for the next step in your hands.

More third paragraphs

Let's take a look at some generic third paragraphs.

Smaller firm

"I am especially interested in Yourco because I have found small but growing firms to provide professional satisfaction and broad responsibilities.

My exposure to small firms as customers and suppliers has convinced me that a firm like Yourco provides the mix of professionalism, challenge and commitment that I seek in my next job."

Larger firm

"My exploration of potential employers has indicated that moving to a larger firm with greater product variety and market clout would be a natural step in my marketing career.

Yourco is particularly attractive to me because of the excellent training program you offer and the multitude of career opportunities that a large firm can provide."

Relocation

"My interest in Yourco developed from my exploration of opportunities in the Chicago area, where I will be moving in September."

Change of field/industry

"Yourco is attractive to me because I can utilize the talents I developed at Nowco in a different and more robust industry."

"I am interested in Dollarco because it provides an opportunity to pursue my interest in marketing with a firm that sells a service in which I am expert—financial services."

Chapter 6

Closing: Road to an Opening

•••

In this chapter, the JSC will learn to write a good fourth paragraph, a closing that keeps the control of the job-search process in their own hands.

The ball is in your court

We had completed our sessions on the first three paragraphs of a cover letter, and the Job Search Club was discussing the best way to close.

"Hire me!" Gabrielle joked, "Then I won't have to write any more cover letters."

"At least read my cover letter," suggested Harry.

"Too much, and then too little," I offered. "Almost no one gets hired based on correspondence. On the other hand, if the employer just reads your correspondence, you won't really be satisfied. What you really want is to arrange a job interview."

"Okay," said Lauren joining in. "But isn't that obvious? Why else would you be writing?"

"Not necessarily. The person receiving your letter gets all kinds of correspondence every day," I responded. "Besides, even when it is obvious, it pays to be explicit when you want your thoughts to be clear."

Sensing that we were ready, I asked each member to write a closing paragraph so we could test our principles in practice. David offered this:

•••

David's draft closing

"The enclosed resume will give you more details about the skills I can bring to your firm. If you agree that I would be a good candidate, I would welcome the opportunity to meet with you personally to explore the possible contributions I can make to Happy Company. Thank you for your time and consideration."

•••

Gabrielle: Your paragraph certainly reads smoothly, but I am still concerned. Couldn't you make it a little shorter? For example, the first sentence could be simply: "My resume is enclosed."

David: I am trying to get them interested in reading my resume.

Gabrielle: If she or he isn't interested after the first three paragraphs, promising "more details" is probably not an inducement. Besides, you have missed the point of a resume. A good resume is not an accumulation of details; it's a presentation of the positive characteristics you have demonstrated, achieved or learned in some context, like a job or student club.

Don't try to win on the last pitch

Gabrielle is correct. Some job-seekers try to achieve their objective in the last few sentences. But if the first three paragraphs were good, that isn't a necessary task for the fourth. If they weren't good, an offer of more details on the resume isn't likely to help.

Harry: I tend to agree with Gabrielle, but I am more concerned about your second sentence. It seems so passive. All you've said is that you would welcome the opportunity to meet with him or her. You could be a bit more assertive.

David: I see your point. But what do you suggest?

Harry: How about this: "Next week I will call you to see if a meeting can be arranged."

David: That seems a bit forward.

Harry: But it's not overly forward, and it's certainly not rude.

Keep the ball in your court

Harry is making a good point here. Closing with a promise to call the person receiving your letter has two major advantages for you as a jobseeker":

- You can convey to the reader that you are a person who has initiative and follow-through—two critical skills in business.

- You keep the ball in your court. Since the next move is up to you, you don't need to sit and wait for a reply. That reality is good for your morale, an important element of a job search. In addition, your call may increase the probability of your being interviewed.

Gabrielle: David, I think you can reconsider your last sentence, too. Thanking someone for their time and consideration in a letter, before you know they've given you any time or consideration, seems nice but hardly necessary.

David thought about the feedback he had received from the JSC and decided to write a shorter, more proactive closing paragraph.

• •

David's revised closing

"My resume is enclosed. Next week I will contact your office to see if a meeting can be arranged at your convenience. Thank you."

• •

The JSC members agreed that this seemed like a good closing paragraph, so we decided to spend a little time on drafting some other possible closings.

"My resume is enclosed. On November 10, I will contact your office to arrange a meeting to discuss career opportunities for me at Sundance Marketing."

Some people find it helpful to indicate the date they will call the potential employer. This date is usually between one and two weeks after your letter is mailed. Many people are reluctant to call an employer, so specifying a particular date in your letter reduces the chance that you will put off your call until tomorrow (and tomorrow and tomorrow).

"I would like the opportunity to meet with you to discuss career possibilities for me at Computer Designs International. A resume highlighting my work experience and academic background is enclosed. I will contact your office next week to arrange a meeting at your convenience."

A good closing. If you are going to say more about your resume than the fact that it is enclosed, it is a good idea to mention work experience before academic background. Academics would be more important to your professors, but the term "work experience" would be more appealing to a potential employer.

"I am eager to explore career opportunities with you. On February 8, I will contact your office to arrange a meeting at your convenience. Thank you."

Short, but not abrupt. This is a good closing, too.

"My resume is enclosed. I would like to pursue career possibilities for me with Northwest Outfitters. On March 30, I will contact your office to arrange a meeting."

This closing is acceptable, but it would be better to add "at your convenience" to the end of the last sentence. Being assertive is just fine, but seeming presumptuous is not really to your advantage.

"I will be in Atlanta from January 12 to 20 and I am eager to meet with you in person. Next week, I will call you to see if we can arrange a meeting during that time."

This is a good closing for a person seeking a job in a distant location. Letting the employer know that you will be in Atlanta lets him/her know that you are at least reasonably serious about relocating. It also makes it clear that you don't expect the firm to cover travel costs (they probably wouldn't anyway) and may tug at the reader's heartstrings a bit (you are making a special trip). If the purpose of your visit is largely to pursue career opportunities, be sure to mention it. For example "I will be in Atlanta from January 12 to 20 to explore career possibilities."

Anthony raised a good question: "You have encouraged us to be proactive. What do you do if there is no one to call. An obvious example would be a response to a help-wanted ad that gives no name." Anthony had a point. In some job search situations you can identify the name of a particular person, but often you can't. In those cases, you can close like this:

"My resume is enclosed. May I look forward to hearing from you about a job interview?"

Cecily followed up with another question related to help-wanted ads: "I know that most jobs are not found through want ads, but some are. What should you do if the ad says that a salary history or salary expectations is an absolute requirement?"

I shared two thoughts with Cecily in that regard.

You could decide not to provide the information. After all, the request is either a mechanism for screening people out or a disguised attempt by the firm to do a salary survey.

You could decide to respond in one of several ways:

"My salary expectation is consistent with the market trend."

Or:

"I am sure that your salary offer would be competitive and I look forward to discussing this matter at a job interview."

Or:

"My salary expectations are in the mid-40s to mid-50s, depending on the overall package."

In terms of salary history you could say:

"I will be happy to discuss the details of my salary history at a job interview," and give a range for your current and/or previous jobs.

Where are we now?

In this chapter, we learned how to write a short closing paragraph that keeps the initiative for follow-up in your hands. In the next chapter, we will see what the JSC learns by drafting an entire cover letter.

Chapter 7

•••

Writing a
Prototype

•••

Early in this book we saw how members of the Job Search Club researched a career, an industry and a particular firm (Chapter 2). Then we followed the JSC as they drafted and discussed each of the four key paragraphs in a cover letter (Chapters 3 through 6).

In the next two chapters, we will see how each of the members of the Job Search Club writes a cover letter s/he can use as a prototype for letters to many employers. In Chapter 7, two JSC members will start from scratch, write a prototype and then individualize it by modular construction. In Chapter 8, we will see how six other prototypes were developed. To help you find an approach that facilitates writing your own cover letters, the JSC members have used several different approaches for organizing their thoughts. In addition, we will avoid showing you cases of an "obvious candidate"—a person whose background so closely matches what a firm is seeking that she would be a strong candidate for an interview even without a good cover letter. My intent is to help you write cover letters that will obtain interviews even when you are not an obvious candidate.

You can benefit in three ways from this chapter. First, you will see the process of putting together an entire letter. Second, the cover letters the JSC members write may serve as examples for your own letters. Third, you will see how to move from a prototype to a letter for a specific employer, a process you can repeat for hundreds of employers.

Starting to write

"I'm psyched," Lauren announced at the next Job Search Club meeting. "Let's start writing."

"I'm glad you are so enthused," I told her, "but let's pause for a moment and do a little thinking." As the following story illustrates, it makes sense to do some planning before you start writing.

••

Learning from Rodin: Plan

One thing life teaches us is that knowledge and wisdom don't fit neatly into tight little categories. For example, the great sculptor Rodin can help us write our cover letters.

Picture Rodin creating "The Thinker." Did he just take his clay and make an image of somebody sitting with his fist under his chin? Of course not.

Rodin gathered his tools and materials. He sketched out his plan for the work he wanted to create. With that preparation complete, Rodin could proceed to create, his tools nearby and his plan at his hand.

Is this approach slower than putting down a glob of clay and then modeling it? Probably, but the result is much more impressive.

••

Gabrielle asked the next logical question: "What should we have at hand before we start writing?" I suggested this short list to her:

- The positive characteristics you offer that the firm needs.
- Your motivation for a particular kind of job, firm and/or industry.
- Some ideas about demonstrating communication skills.
- A list of possible credibility gaps and ideas to close them.

Most of this information you should have gathered already when you researched a particular career and a specific industry. Research about a given firm will probably need to be done when you are about to seek a job with that firm. (See Chapter 2.)

Gabrielle's draft

Gabrielle was the first one to present the group with a draft. She decided that this would be her "financial analysis" draft and that she would write it as though it was designed for a particular employer, in this case Dollarco. Following a process like David's in Chapter 2, Gabrielle constructed a financial analysis research chart. Then she identified those of her positive characteristics (skills) an employer might need in a financial analyst. Next, Gabrielle identified some sound motives for wanting the job by constructing an I want/the employer offers chart (Chapter 5). Gabrielle also kept in mind the potential credibility gap caused by her absence from the full-time professional work force for the last 10 years (Chapter 1). Now that she had a plan for her letter, this is what Gabrielle wrote:

The Job Search Club members looked at Gabrielle's draft and asked her some questions about it.

Bill: The first thing you told the JSC was that you have been out of the full-time, professional work force for 10 years. Yet that fact is the last thing you mentioned in your letter. Why?

Gabrielle: A major purpose of the cover letter is to obtain an interview by showing what you can do for the firm. So I started with my strengths. There was only one reason to mention my 10-year gap at all: to explain the gap that will appear

Gabrielle's prototype text

986 Linden Blvd.
Elkhart, IN 46515

February 8, 1997

Ms. Florence McNeil
Vice President-Finance
Dollarco, Inc.
7316 Lafollette Blvd.
Indianapolis, IN 46263

Dear Ms. McNeil:

As an experienced professional with excellent quantitative skills, I am interested in becoming a financial analyst at Dollarco. I am attracted to your firm because of the praise you have received in *The Wall Street Journal* and from professionals I have met in seven years as a financial analyst.

Here are some of the abilities I can contribute to Dollarco:

> **Corporate experience:** Five years in the finance department of Milwaukee Power and two years in the treasury department at Cheese Products, Inc.

> **Research:** Proven ability to find sources, ask the right questions and evaluate the implications of data.

> **Communications skills:** Received praise from employers for written reports and oral presentations.

> **Familiarity with leasing services:** Gained through recent work experience.

A career in financial analysis with Dollarco appeals to me for several reasons. First, I would enjoy using my quantitative and analytical skills in a business where financial expertise is critical to success. Second, the leasing industry is particularly interesting to me. As *Dollar Today* magazine put it, "Leasing may be the wave of the future in a rapidly changing world." Third, my research indicates that Dollarco has the kind of working environment where I can succeed professionally.

I hope that we can meet to discuss the contributions I can make to Dollarco, even if you don't have a position available at present. Because child-rearing responsibilities are no longer a factor, I am eager to resume my career as a financial analyst. Next week I will call you to arrange for a meeting at your convenience.

Sincerely yours,

Gabrielle Feldman

Gabrielle Feldman

in my resume in terms of professional experience. I didn't want the reader to be confused or to think that I was trying to hide something on that score. Although there is no need to apologize for my absence from the profession, mentioning it early in the letter isn't likely to help me any.

Some knowledgeable people would suggest making no comment at all about absence from the labor market. If you follow that suggestion, make sure your resume includes an explanation. For example, "Temporarily left work force to raise young children."

Gabrielle is making a solid point here: If something needs to be said, but isn't a selling point, don't make it an early or prominent part of your letter.

Lauren: How did you determine the points you wanted to make in your second paragraph?

Gabrielle: I followed our general principle: What do I offer that the employer needs? Experience in the field is always an attraction, so I mentioned that first. Research and communication are important skills, so I mentioned them second. Since Dollarco is in the leasing business, I wanted to show familiarity with that field.

David: Why mention your leasing experience last? It seems it should go first since that's a direct connection to Dollarco.

Gabrielle: I had to think strategically on that one. On the one hand, I do have familiarity with leasing, and it's current. On the other, my position is administrative and the job is part-time. That combination tells me to make the statement, but not in a lead-off position.

Harry: To follow up on David's question, do you consider the statement about leasing misleading?

Gabrielle: Not at all. I stated only the truth, familiarity with leasing. Further, I indicated a "recent work experience," which is true. I didn't claim I was a financial analyst there.

David: I am interested in knowing how you identified the items for the "why I want to work for you" paragraph.

Gabrielle: I wanted to show a reason based on each of three factors: the type of job, the industry and the particular firm. The first point, the job, required the most thought because I had to show succinctly that I was realistically motivated—namely, what I wanted really comes with the job. The other two points (the firm, the industry) were easier for me because they flowed from research about what other people had said.

David: I notice that you referred to several publications in your letter. Why?

Gabrielle: By showing that I had researched the industry and the firm, I was showing that I am thorough and seriously motivated. Mentioning a trade journal read by many financial analysts helps them see me more as one of them rather than as an outsider.

David: Let me follow up on my previous question. Since you haven't worked for the firm, how could you truthfully speak about the working environment at Dollarco?

Gabrielle: I learned about Dollarco from an informational interview with someone in the finance department (see Chapter 11). In the case of some larger firms, I might find articles in a magazine (*Fortune* or *Working Woman*, for example) or a book (*The 100 Best Companies to Work for in America*), which talk about working environment. If I didn't have a reliable source of information and/or I didn't believe that working environment is an important consideration, I wouldn't mention it.

Gabrielle has made two good points in her discussion with David. First, when possible, try to show a motivation connected with one or more of these factors: job, firm, industry. Second, unless you have a sound basis for making a statement, it doesn't belong in your letter.

Moving to modular

The JSC was satisfied that Gabrielle had a solid basis for what she had written for Dollarco and that it would make a good prototype for any cover letter dealing with financial analysis. Now we needed to see how a prototype text could be used for cover letters to many potential employers. We started with some alternate situations for Gabrielle to address.

Situation: same industry, different firm

Gabrielle: Most of my letter can remain as is. I would need two changes.

1. First paragraph:
The reference to praise in *The Wall Street Journal* is specific to Dollarco, so that has to be removed. I could replace it with a statement from my research about the leasing industry. More difficult, but not impossible, would be a statement from my research about each firm in particular.

2. Closing paragraph:
My sentence about the working environment is specific to Dollarco, so it has to be removed. I could replace it with a statement about each particular firm. If that proved too difficult, I could make a statement about enjoying the work environment leasing firms often provide. That statement could be based on informational meetings, articles in the press or my part-time job with a leasing firm.

Situation: different industry, firm, same type of job

Gabrielle: I could combine the changes we just discussed with some changes to reflect a new industry. I can still use the same basic draft. After all, most of the letter is a function of the type of job I want, and that is staying the same.

Gabrielle is making an important point about prototype cover letters. Most of your letter revolves around one topic. For Gabrielle, it's the type of job. For someone else, it might be a certain industry, like hospitality or transportation. As long as your main topic is the same, you can use the same prototype for writing letters to many firms.

To illustrate how modular construction can work, Gabrielle revised her text to reflect a changed situation. In the letter on page 81, she is still applying to be a financial analyst, but this time Gabrielle is writing to a different firm in a different industry.

Do the changes ring true?

After we looked over the Drinkco text together, Bill wanted to ask Gabrielle some questions.

Bill: I would like to see if your changes have resulted in a strong letter. In the first paragraph, you write about financial analysts you have met, instead of the reference to *The Wall Street Journal* in your prototype.

Gabrielle: It's not always possible to know what type of statement would be the strongest. As the Bible says, "We know in part and prophesize in part." Therefore, I wanted a strong statement to indicate that my interest in the firm is based on something substantial. Whether professional reputation or a comment in *The Wall Street Journal* would appeal more to a particular reader is hard to know. In any event, I didn't have a specific published source to refer to for Drinkco the way I had for Dollarco.

Bill: How about in paragraph two: What were you thinking when you wrote "familiarity with the consumer products industry"?

Gabrielle: In the "why you should interview me" paragraph, you want to tie yourself as closely to the firm's needs as possible. Therefore, I used a construct, "consumer products," which covers both Drinkco and my experience at Cheese Products.

Gabrielle has made two good points here. First, you will seldom be certain as to what statement will be the most compelling to any given reader. Your job is to make sure that any statement you do make is a point in your favor. If you write a credible sentence and have a sound rationale behind it, you have probably helped your case. Second, try to find a reasonable construct that allows you to link your past experience to your next job.

Lauren: Is that why you mentioned Cheese Products before Milwaukee Power in the first part of the second paragraph?

Gabrielle: Yes. I changed the order of the facts to put the most powerful fact first.

Bill: Let's move on to the third paragraph, "why I want to work for you." You made two changes there.

Gabrielle: Yes, remember both the industry and the firm have changed for this letter and I wanted to make a connection to both. By citing *Business News*, I am showing that I've done my homework. Even better, this particular quotation ties the industry to my field of professional interest. My reference to the struggle against the

Gabrielle's revised text
(new sentences are underlined)

986 Linden Blvd.
Elkhart, IN 46515

February 8, 1997

Mr. Frank Antonelli
Financial Vice President
Drinkco, Inc.
2459 Straw Square
Indianapolis, IN 46268

Dear Mr. Antonelli:

As an experienced professional with excellent quantitative skills, I am interested in joining Drinkco as a financial analyst. <u>This is a field in which I developed a high level of skill in the course of seven years' professional experience.</u>

Here are some of the abilities I can contribute to Drinkco:

Corporate experience: Two years in the treasury at Cheese Products, Inc., preceded my five years in the finance department of Milwaukee Power.

Research: Proven ability to find sources, ask the right questions and evaluate the implications of data.

Communications skills: Received praise from employers for written reports and oral presentations.

Familiarity with leasing services: <u>The challenges faced by Cheese Products, Inc., are similar to those you face at Drinkco. The importance of sound financial management to ensure resources for marketing and production is a challenge I relish.</u>

A career in financial analysis with Drinkco appeals to me for several reasons. First, I would enjoy using my quantitative and analytical skills in a business where financial expertise is critical to success. <u>Second, the importance of finance to the beverage industry is attractive to me. As *Business News* reported, "The beverage industry is realizing that its ability to bring goods to market is tied to getting its financial house in order." Third, I want to be part of a company that is struggling against the beverage giants.</u>

I hope that we can meet to discuss the contributions I can make to Drinkco, even if you don't have a position available at present. Since my child-rearing responsibilities are no longer a factor, I am eager to resume my career as a financial analyst. Next week I will call you to arrange for a meeting at your convenience.

Sincerely yours,

Gabrielle Feldman

Gabrielle Feldman
Enclosure: Resume

industry giants was framed in terms of my interest in the firm. That statement is credible even though I couldn't say anything about Drinkco's particular role in that struggle.

••

Gabrielle is planning to return to the work force after a 10-year absence. That requires leaping a significant hurdle. Notice that Gabrielle plans to return to a field in which she had been professionally established — in this case, financial analysis. It is generally easier to clear one hurdle rather than two. So it will be easier for Gabrielle to return as a financial analyst than to try an entirely new profession.

••

Lauren's letter

After our discussion with Gabrielle, we looked at Lauren's prototype text.

In the letter on page 84, Lauren is seeking to move ahead in her current profession, one of several options she is considering.

After the JSC members read Lauren's prototype, several members had comments or questions.

Gabrielle: I notice that you didn't give your current title or the name of your company. Was there a reason?

Lauren: I wanted to emphasize my professional experience in marketing to draw a connection between my professional past and my desired future. In this case, my title as "Senior Research Analyst" might be more of a distraction than an asset. Similarly, I wanted to indicate my experience in consumer products, since that category fits both Specialty Cereals and the firm where I work now. Naming my current employer, which makes rubber bands, would not strengthen that connection.

Some of my friends leave out their job title and company name to preserve the confidentiality of their job search. I did not feel that reason applied to my case, but it's something anyone who currently has a job needs to consider.

David: You told us once that you have an MBA. Why didn't you mention it?

Lauren: What is most useful for me in obtaining an interview will be my work experience. The MBA helped me get my current job and what I learned in the program has served me well. But college degrees become less significant as work experience increases in value. The graduate degree is on my resume, but it is not so important that it needs to be highlighted or reframed in my cover letter.

Lauren is showing good insight. Experience in a field is usually more important than a graduate degree. If Lauren felt the MBA might be important to the reader, she could mention the degree without emphasizing it. Many people shoot themselves in the foot by thinking that an MBA or other graduate degree is a sure-fire door opener. On the other hand, if a certain degree is required, make sure to mention that you have it in the first or second paragraph.

Harry: How did you determine the selling points you wanted to make in the second paragraph, "why you should interview me"?

Lauren: My basic theme is that I am an experienced marketing professional who is ready to move up. To support that theme, I wanted to show some of my marketing accomplishments and some of the other skills I would need in product management.

Harry: To pursue that last point, the example you give for communication skills is taken from the nonprofessional sphere of your life. Did you have a reason?

Lauren: Communication skills are very important for a product manager, but I really don't get to use them on my current job. My choice was to show a credible avocational context or not mention the talent. I chose the newspaper and the Chamber of Commerce because they are credible examples of an important positive characteristic. It was better to include an example that is strong but not the very strongest rather than ignore mentioning the skill completely.

David: Where did you come-up with the Yum-Yum Breakfast Club?

Lauren: Remember, we want to draw a connection between ourselves and the prospective employer. An interest in their product is one way to do that. I included this point because it is useful. I placed it last because it is not central to my letter.

Gabrielle: In your third paragraph, "why I want to work for you," you draw two connections to the firm (*The Wall Street Journal* article; medium-sized firm) but none to the job or the industry. What was your thinking?

Lauren: It is important to use your own judgment when applying the job, firm, industry guideline Richard gave us for this paragraph. Mentioning my avocational interest in cereal in paragraph two addresses the industry aspect. Unfortunately, I haven't yet researched the business aspects of the cereal industry enough to make an intelligent statement about it. I had to make the most out of what I had available when it was time to write.

I see your point about the value of mentioning my motivation for product management. Perhaps I could have added a sentence like "My interest in product management stems from my desire to combine my talents in research, communication and organizing in the broader context that product management offers a marketing professional" or "I am interested in product management because it would be the next logical step in my marketing career."

After we reviewed Lauren's prototype letter, we were convinced that it was ready to be amended as needed for other letters. The JSC members gave Lauren a variety of situations to deal with.

Different company, same industry

Lauren: Most of the letter can stay as it is. Obviously, the name of the firm changes in the first paragraph. In the third paragraph, I would either refer to my research about this firm or write a generic statement about my interest in the industry. If this firm is not medium-sized, a situation I mentioned in my prototype, I'd refer to my attraction to the firm's philosophy, track record or geography.

Harry: Would a generic statement about the industry be a substitute for your statement about the Yum-Yum Breakfast Club?

Lauren: Only in terms of space utilization. That was an avocational statement showing a connection from the heart. My statements about the industry would be from a business perspective.

Lauren's prototype text

1436 Twin City Center
St. Paul, MN 54144

February 1, 1997

Mr. Bill Iron
Vice President, Marketing
Specialty Cereals, Inc.
1234 Fifth Ave.
Battle Creek, MI 10098

Dear Mr. Iron:

I am interested in joining Specialty Cereals, Inc., as a product manager. My interest in this field has developed in the course of my marketing experience with a consumer products firm over the last five years. Some of the qualifications I can offer your company are:

A solid knowledge of marketing. I have spent several years analyzing marketing data and working with managers to bring projects from inception to completion.

A record of accomplishment. For example, in my current position I have played a key role in establishing two new products as serious competitors in their field.

An ambition to succeed. I have been promoted three times in four years.

Excellent communication skills, both written and oral. I write a monthly column for a community newspaper and have given numerous presentations to the Chamber of Commerce.

A long-standing avocational interest in cereals. For two years I was an officer of the Yum-Yum Breakfast Club.

A career in product management with Specialty Cereals would be very appealing to me. It would enable me to pursue my interest in this field with a company praised by *The Wall Street Journal* as "a shining light in the world of consumer marketing." In addition, I wish to work for a medium-sized company since that is an environment I have found conducive to gaining a broad perspective on an entire functional area.

My resume is enclosed. On February 8, I will contact your office to see if a meeting can be arranged at your convenience. Thank you.

Sincerely yours,

Lauren Giovanni

Lauren Giovanni

Different product—toys

Lauren: The core of my letter is about marketing as a profession and I don't need to change that part. In addition, toys are still a consumer product, so that term in the first paragraph is still appropriate.

The second paragraph requires a change. I still need to delete the sentence about Yum-Yum. If I have gained professional insights into toys or children's products I could mention it. I might write:

••

"Knowledge of key aspects of the toy industry—based on extensive research into consumer demographics."

••

Thank goodness you helped me add a sentence about product management to the third paragraph of my prototype! That should be a constant in all my letters, unless I am seeking a different kind of job. If possible, I should write a line or two regarding what I like about toys, that particular company, the firm's track record or my attraction to its location.

David: What if you were looking for a different kind of job?

Lauren: As long as I am writing about marketing, I can use this prototype. If I want to seek a different profession, I would write a different prototype first. Then I could change pieces of it to reflect different firms or industries.

David: You told us earlier that you were considering a move to the nonprofit sector. How would that affect your letter?

Lauren: I still want to be a marketing professional, so the changes would reflect the particular organization ("firm") and the nonprofit sector ("industry").

In the "why you should interview me" paragraph, I would delete the characteristic of ambition and replace it with a statement of my desire to be of service. Avocational interest in a particular cause would replace Yum-Yum Breakfast Club.

In the third paragraph, I would explain why I want to apply my talents to that particular cause and the value of satisfaction I would gain. If I could find a reference to that particular organization in the press, I would use it.

Following our discussion, Lauren made changes on her prototype product manager letter to reflect a change from a cereals firm to a toys firm.

Computers, job search and your cover letter

So far, the Job Search Club has been developing their cover letter with the traditional paper format in mind. Lauren asked a question that brought us to our next topic: communication by computer. "Doesn't that change the whole ball game?" she asked. "Not really," I replied. "It's more like playing baseball on astroturf in a domed stadium rather than on grass in a traditional ballpark."

Lauren and the Job Search Club wanted to be convinced, so I identified the changes computers are making in job searches and the implications for cover letters.

Lauren's toy industry text
(new sentences are underlined)

1436 Twin City Center
St. Paul, MN 54144

February 1, 1997

Ms. Roberta Steel
Vice President, Marketing
Toddler Toys, Inc.
5678 Playland Rd.
Providence, RI 02768

Dear Ms. Steel:

I am interested in joining Toddler Toys, Inc., as a product manager. My interest in this field has developed in the course of my marketing experience with a consumer products firm over the last five years. Some of the qualifications I can offer your company are:

A solid knowledge of marketing. I have spent several years analyzing marketing data and working with managers to bring projects from inception to completion.

A record of accomplishment. For example, in my current position I have played a key role in establishing two new products as serious competitors in their field.

An ambition to succeed. I have been promoted three times in four years.

Excellent communication skills, both written and oral. I write a monthly column for a community newspaper and have given numerous presentations to the Chamber of Commerce.

Knowledge of key aspects of the toy industry, based on extensive research into consumer demographics.

My interest in product management stems from my desire to utilize my talents in the broader context that the position offers a marketing professional. I am interested in the toy industry in particular because of the unique challenge posed by having children as consumers but having adults paying the bills. By the way, I have family in New England, so relocating poses no problem.

My resume is enclosed. On February 8, I will contact your office to see if a meeting can be arranged at your convenience. Thank you.

Sincerely yours,

Lauren Giovanni

Lauren Giovanni
Enclosure: Resume

Scanning

Many firms, particularly large ones, are scanning job applications in order to deal more effectively with the large volume they receive. Here is a simple but functional description of what happens:

Your resume will be read by an optical scanning device (referred to as an "OCR") that stores your resume (and thousands of others) in computer memory as a data file. The traditional approach is to read applications with human eyes and file them in folders (or file them in trash cans!). In large-volume situations, scanning is not really less personal than having your resume and cover letter read by a harassed human being.

Your cover letter: Here things are a bit more uncertain. A cover letter might be scanned much like a resume. In some cases, it may be discarded.

What does scanning mean for you? As several authors have noted, it directly affects the way you write your resume, because scanners are oriented to nouns rather than verbs. The appendix notes several books on that subject.

Scanning doesn't really change the substance of your letter at all. If it is scanned, it remains a partner to your resume. If it is not scanned, it probably wouldn't have been read by a human being either. Because you have already developed a prototype, the time cost for sending a cover letter is minimal. Because you don't know if your letter will be scanned, the risk of not sending it is considerable.

Harry raised a reasonable question. "Are you saying that nothing has changed because of scanning?" he asked. "No," I replied. "My point is that scanning changes mostly the way large firms store and retrieve information about job applicants. The implications for your cover letter are more limited: First, your letter should be more oriented to nouns than to verbs. Second, the use of industry or professional acronyms and buzzwords makes more sense because they help you score more "hits" during a computer search of stored applications. Third, because of the way data is retrieved by the firm, your cover letter may be read after the resume, rather than first. Even if it is read second, a well-written letter will still increase your probability of winning the job interview.

How this chapter helps

We saw how two people wrote, reviewed and refined a prototype cover letter. Rather than starting afresh when writing to a new employer, both Lauren and Gabrielle were able to change a few sentences of the prototype to reflect changing situations.

Some points to remember are:

- Plan your letter before you start writing. That includes some serious thought about your positive characteristics, motivation and potential credibility gap(s).

- When mentioning more than one point, rank-order them in the reader's anticipated order of interest. This is especially true for paragraphs two and three.

- Indicate the research you did for that letter. Research lends credibility to your letter.

When in doubt:

- Include a strong statement, even if it isn't the most compelling point possible.
- Write nothing unless you are sure your statement is both accurate and true.
- Try to link your past experience (and behavior) to your next job as clearly as possible. Finding a common construct that covers both a past job and your desired future is one good way to do that.

In the next chapter, we will see how six other JSC members developed their own prototype cover letters.

Chapter 8

••

Seven Pillars of Writing Wisdom

••

Learning from the efforts of Lauren and Gabrielle, the other members of the Job Search Club wrote their own prototype cover letters. Each had a distinct situation to address and none were obvious candidates for the kind of job they wanted. Their letters and the accompanying comments will help you with your own text.

Downsizing

Cecily came to see me with deep concern. A competent professional, she thought she would always have a place in customer service at Calco Computer Corp. Unfortunately, Calco was "downsizing"—a euphemism for laying off workers. "I never thought I would have to look for another job," Cecily said to me. "In three weeks I will be out on the street. I'm just not ready for this."

It was easy to empathize with Cecily. She had done everything right for her employer and now she felt terribly wronged. But tea and sympathy are not enough. We had to get to work landing Cecily's next job.

Our first step was to remove some burdens that Cecily shouldn't continue to bear. One was panic. Cecily had heard that it is easier to get a job when you still have a job—and she had only three weeks left. I explained to her that there was much less truth in that notion today than in the past. With so many people losing jobs because of downsizing or business failures, being out of work no longer carries the stigma it once did.

The second burden was doubt about her worth. "If they don't need me at Calco, where I have worked for years, who is going to need me somewhere else?" Cecily thought to herself. I told Cecily that Calco paid people because their services were needed. Since she had been retained by Calco for many years, she produced something of value to earn her salary. What's more, some of what she demonstrated, achieved or learned for Calco would be attractive to her next employer.

I reminded Cecily that, like everyone else, her basic task was to convey, clearly and concisely, these four points:

1. Positive characteristics of importance to the employer.

2. Motivation.

3. Communication ability.

4. Bridging the credibility gap.

Her experience at Calco could help Cecily present the first three points very well. The fourth point, the credibility gap, was not insurmountable. I suggested that we plan her letter by constructing a chart for each point. We assumed for this letter that Cecily would pursue similar work, but in a different industry.

For the sake of this exercise, Cecily wrote to a company that manufactures hand tools. Let's see what Cecily had to say.

Cecily's planning chart

Key ideas:	Employer wants: (based on career research)	I offer:
Positive characteristics	• Business sense. • Organization. • Thoroughness.	Give examples from professional context; show results.
Motivation	• Job: • Firm: • Industry:	• Enjoy it; continue career. • Situation specific. • Situation specific.
Communication	• Written and oral.	• Staff meetings. • Phone work. • Written reports. • Quality cover letter.
	Employer will be concerned that I:	Addressed by:
Credibility Gap	• Am set in my ways. • Won't learn new product or service.	• Show flexibility or adjustment to new situations. • Rapid mastery of product knowledge.

Cecily has demonstrated some sound strategic thinking. When you are making a career transition, it is usually advisable to set up as few hurdles as possible. In this case, for example, Cecily is looking for a new employer in a new industry, but in a similar type of job. Thus, she has a visible connection to her next employer (kind of job) and two hurdles to leap (employer, industry). Two hurdles are easier than three and one strong connection is better than none.

A strong opening is a good idea. Cecily's clearest strength is her experience in customer service and she lets the reader know about it right away.

The second paragraph highlights positive characteristics Cecily has shown in her professional experience that an employer needs. She has shown her business sense by referring to customers, profitability and not taking time away from line managers. In addition, Cecily addressed a potential credibility gap by showing her ability to quickly master knowledge of new products.

Cecily's letter

2468 Ponce Street
Philadelphia, PA 19153

January 6, 1997

Theodore Young
Vice President, Administration
Handy-Wrench, Inc.
1313 Hammerville Drive
Clark, New Jersey 07066

Dear Mr. Young:

As an experienced customer service manager, I am interested in bringing my skill and energy to Handy-Wrench, Inc. Let me tell you what I can contribute to your firm:

Experience: Dealt with the stress of satisfying corporate customers whose business is critical to the profitability of my current employer.

Efficiency: Because of my organizational ability, customers usually had a response to their inquiries within the hour.

Problem solving: In many cases, solved customer problems without taking time from line managers.

Communication: Wrote reports for management summarizing customer concerns and suggesting possible solutions.

Product knowledge: Mastered the intricacies of computer products and applications within weeks. Remain current with new developments in the field.

A position in customer service with Handy-Wrench would be very attractive to me. I enjoy this field because of its daily challenges and its importance to the company's success. Handy-Wrench is especially appealing to me because of my interest in the "Tool Designed for Today" approach your annual report discusses.

My resume is enclosed. I will call you next week to see if a brief meeting can be arranged.

Sincerely yours,

Cecily Fine

Cecily Fine

Enclosure

Cecily's third paragraph is especially important because she indicates why she wants to work for this particular employer (Handy-Wrench). The fact that she researched the firm also shows a professional mind-set.

What if Cecily writes a letter after her last day of work at Calco? No problem. Most of the letter can stay the same. In the second paragraph Cecily can refer to "a business much like yours" instead of writing "my current employer."

When writing to other firms about her interest in the same field, only the third paragraph will need substantial change. If Cecily has done her research in this industry and field, she should be able to identify something to say about each particular firm without an enormous amount of additional research.

Jeannette

Jeannette was a recent college graduate. She had majored in accounting and was interested in pursuing a business career where she could use her analytical skills. Although she was interested in several possible fields, we decided to focus on financial analysis for her first letter. Though Jeannette was a recent graduate, she had to address the same four points as Cecily. To help her plan her letter, Jeannette drew a chart like the one below.

Jeannette realized that she wasn't going to be an obvious candidate for the job she wanted. She had never worked in financial analysis, even part-time. She had never been class president or earned a 4.0 GPA. However, she also realized that getting the interview would depend in part on her cover letter. Jeannette knew that the quality of her cover letter was one way to gain favorable recognition compared with her competitors. A clear, concise expression of her ability to meet an employer's needs—her positive characteristics and a well-considered motivation—would be important factors in getting invited to an interview.

Jeannette's planning chart

Key ideas:	Employer wants: (based on career research)	I offer:
Positive characteristics	• Analytical for cash flow.	• Analyzed reasons (class projects).
	• Problem solving.	• Solved student's conflicts.
	• Team Player.	• Work hard, on time.
Motivation	• Job:	• Apply talents; how interest developed.
	• Firm:	• Situation specific; but learning and career growth a possibility.
	• Industry:	• Presentations in class; term papers; quality cover letter.
	Employer will be concerned that I:	Addressed by:
Credibility gap	• Lack financial analysis experience.	• Have positive characteristics.
	• Am just looking for any job.	• Show attraction to specific situation.
	• Am not mobile.	• Will relocate.

Eager to write a perfect cover letter, Jeannette said she would be meticulous and make sure that every word she put on paper would be just right. I said I hoped not.

Jeannette: But don't we need to write a dynamite cover letter?

Richard: Yes. The final product should be as perfect as you can make it. But your initial draft should just get your thoughts down on paper.

The draft cover letter Jeannette wrote appears on page 94. The brackets indicate what Jeannette would do to make her letter appropriate to a specific firm.

When Jeannette brought in her draft, we developed a checklist as a guide for identifying possible improvements.

- Did I show my positive characteristics in the best possible light?
- Is my motivation clear?
- Is my letter a good example of my communication skills?
- Have I bridged my credibility gap?

Jeannette wrote her draft in a generic form. That is, she has decided to leave out examples of firm-specific sentences from her prototype. However, she will put firm-specific sentences in the letters she actually sends out.

I reviewed the letter with Jeannette against the criteria we had established and made some suggestions.

Jeannette's checklist

Did Jeannette show her positive characteristics in the best possible light? The first step is to be sure that the characteristics she shows are desired by a prospective employer. In this case Jeannette did have a solid basis for her choices, namely what she had learned from SIGI Plus and informational interviews (Chapters 2 and 11).

The second step is to look at her examples. Are the examples credible? Nothing she has written stretches the truth. Instead, she has given examples that could come from the real life of a recent college graduate. Jeannette has also given examples from several sources—in this case, academics, work and her sorority. Using a variety of sources for your examples is a good idea. (For a more experienced worker, this means pulling examples from more than one job.) One improvement Jeannette can make is an explicit reference to her communication skills. A financial analyst is not just a numbers-cruncher.

Is Jeannette's motivation clear? Part of it is. She lets the reader know that she has researched both her career goal and the particular firm. Further, Jeannette has implicitly demonstrated her seriousness by showing relevant positive characteristics. However, she needs to be careful. She must sure that the particular firm to which she is writing actually has the characteristics she described. Don't use words just because they sound nice.

Jeannette knew the credibility gap she would have to bridge as a recent college graduate. It would have been great to show some related experience, but that wasn't in her background. She has partially bridged this gap by indicating positive characteristics the firm needs that she has, even if they were developed outside of a working environment.

Jeannette's draft prototype

Home Address

Date

Name of Addressee
Firm Address

Dear (Name of Addressee):

As a recent college graduate, I am interested in joining your firm as a financial analyst. My interest in this field has developed as a result of my business classes and meetings with people in the profession.

I am certain that I have the characteristics you need in a new employee:

Analytical ability: Developed through my course work in accounting and finance. Praised by professors for research papers on cash flow analysis and the impact of dividends on working capital.

Problem solving: Solved problems ranging from cash register shrinkage in a retail store to ethnic conflicts on campus.

Reliability: Known as a hard worker who has never missed a deadline at work or in class.

Team player: Brought conflicting viewpoints to a workable conclusion while chairing a campus-wide sorority event.

Before writing to you, I considered my career goals carefully. [Research firm. Then link my goals to what the firm offers]. I am excited about the possibility of contributing my skills and energy to [describe nature of firm, e.g., a young, growing company.]

My resume is enclosed. I will call you next week to see if a meeting can be arranged. I am eager to meet with you and I am prepared to cover the expense of my transportation and lodging for our initial meeting.

Sincerely yours,

Jeannette Ortiz

Jeannette Ortiz

Enclosure

Many people believe that recent graduates "don't know what they want," that they are "just looking for a job—any job." Jeannette has addressed that in part when she showed her motivation for financial analysis. The stronger and clearer that motivation is expressed, the more this part of her credibility gap is closed. If the firm to which she is writing is not near her home or college, she should indicate that she is prepared, perhaps eager, to relocate.

Jeannette's letter is well-organized and strong in content. Her sentences are straightforward and easy to read. Each sentence adds to the message she wants to get across. Jeannette's letter is a very good example of her communication skills. If she makes the changes I suggested, she will be ready to consider her draft a good prototype.

Anthony

Anthony was hoping to move from market research to being an account executive with an advertising agency. His approach to planning a letter differed from Jeannette's. Anthony started by summarizing for himself the theme of his letter: "Experienced marketing professional seeks to take next career step by moving to an advertising agency." Then, he played out a piece of his theme in each of the four paragraphs of his cover letter.

Let's take a look at what Anthony wrote (his letter appears on page 96) and review it.

Anthony started out with a bang by indicating what he offers (marketing experience) and what he wants (account executive). Since his current situation and his next job are closely related, demonstrating his well-considered interest in the marketing field is less important than for a recent college graduate or a person changing fields altogether.

Anthony has also provided some positive reasons for interviewing him. Organizations that provide a professional service often benefit from employing professionals who have been on the client side. Notice that Anthony relates his work history as a positive, rather than saying "although I have never worked in an ad agency...." He also indicates that he has achieved results beyond a narrow expectation of market research. That fact helps bridge the gap between his current job and his next one.

Anthony showed that he is motivated by a positive attraction to a new situation rather than a desire to flee his current one. That approach—focus on the next employer, not leaving the current one—is almost always the best to take. Notice that Anthony indicated an attraction on two bases—the job and the industry. Two good reasons are better than one.

Like Jeannette, Anthony has chosen to make his prototype letter generic to a broad situation—namely, being an account executive in an advertising firm. This text will need some amending before Anthony writes to a specific firm. In the second paragraph, changes for a specific firm might reflect parallels between his current employer and some of the ad agency's clients. That information is available in sources such as the *Standard Directory of Advertising Agencies*, which is found in the reference section of many libraries. Perhaps Anthony could cite something attractive he read about that firm in a trade publication such as *Advertising Age* to add to his third paragraph. Showing that he has researched that particular firm shows a seriousness and thoroughness that employers appreciate.

Anthony's draft prototype

Home Address

Date

Name of Addressee
Firm Address

Dear (Name of Addressee):

As a marketing professional with five years of solid experience, I am interested in joining your firm as an account executive. Although I am happy with my current employer, moving to an advertising agency represents the next logical step in my marketing career.

I can benefit your firm by bringing with me a client-side perspective. As a member of the Ostrich Treats marketing team, I am well aware of the kinds of time, cost and competitive pressures that your clients experience. In addition to my expertise in research, I have applied my findings to solve business problems such as pricing, target markets and advertising theme.

Continuing my career with an advertising agency appeals to me because I want to contribute my skills in research, teamwork and strategy to a diverse clientele. [(Name of Agency) has a particular attraction to me because...]

I hope that we will have a chance to meet personally. Next week, I will call you to see if a meeting can be arranged at your convenience.

Sincerely yours,

Anthony Fontana

Anthony Fontana

Enclosure: Resume

. . . .

David's planning chart

Key ideas:	Employer wants: (based on research)	I offer:
Positive characteristic	• Analytical • Writing • Teamwork • Judgment • Research	• Historical trends. • Latin grammar; zillions of term papers. • Group projects. • Ambiguous situations. • Digger for facts.
Motivation	• Job: • Firm: • Industry:	• Apply talents. • Specific situations. • Historical role of finance in commerce.
Communication	• Written and oral	• Quality of letter. • Solid English. • Helped staff with brief letters on summer job. • Oral presentation and exams.
	Employer will be concerned that I:	Addressed by:
Credibility gap	• Lack career focus • Lack banking personality; not interested in the mundane.	• Show why interested in direction banking. • Show hard-working team player with a pragmatic bent.

David

Like Jeannette, David was a forthcoming college graduate. Unlike Jeannette, David was a liberal arts major concentrating in classics. David wanted a job, not graduate school, but what could he do? Translating Cicero didn't have any apparent attraction to the job market.

I told David that the task was the same for him as for anyone else. David needed to show that he had positive characteristics the firm needed and that his motivation was serious and well-directed. David's liberal arts education could certainly be presented to his advantage if he handled it correctly.

I asked David to identify a field of interest and he mentioned commercial lending for a bank. Then, I asked David to construct a chart to address the four basic points we had discussed at the beginning of this chapter. His chart appears above.

Looking at David's chart we recognized three things:

1. He had many of the positive characteristics needed in a bank lender.
2. David's liberal arts education helped make his claim of good communication skills credible.
3. The credibility gap was a potential Achilles heel, but it could be addressed.

Encouraged by seeing his strengths, but mindful of potential pitfalls, David drafted his text. He is using a generic approach for his draft and indicating items that would be changed to meet specific situations by inserting brackets or blank spaces. Let's read David's draft prototype (on page 99) and then see how it might be improved.

Let's start with the credibility gap. Could David, a student of the classics, convince someone that he has the tools and the motivation to work in an intensely competitive, unsentimental business such as banking? There may be a perception that classics majors are enamored of philosophical issues and would view banking as mundane or even crass.

I believe that the substance of David's letter bridges the gap. He has identified skills needed in banking, indicated that he has researched the field (and will research the firm). Further, David's motivation seems reasonable for a liberal arts major, yet consistent with how the industry might see itself.

As for positive characteristics, he has identified those the bank needs that he offers. Good idea. His examples support the characteristics he claims to have. Further, by referring several times to work experiences, David is showing that he knows that banking does not hire based on academic excellence alone.

How about David's opening line about Cicero? The danger in using a creative opening is the possibility of sounding hokey or apologetic, either of which would turn off most readers.

There are two tests to apply. First, are you reasonably certain that your creativity will be received in a positive way? Second, is the creativity really necessary? Based on those tests, I suggested that David change his opening sentence. What is creative to one person is considered flaky by another. Besides, David had plenty of good characteristics to offer. There was no need to take a risk on an opening that might attract attention in a negative way.

A more prosaic but more effective opening would be: "I am interested in building a career in commercial lending with [name of bank]. Let me tell you how my work experiences and academic studies will help make me an asset to your bank."

Harry: from grocer to broker?

Harry has spent his career managing a supermarket. He has made a comfortable living, but is increasingly uncomfortable with the daily routine for earning it. From Harry's perspective, it is time for a change. I spoke to Harry about where he wanted to go next.

Harry: One thing I am considering is becoming a stockbroker. Slim chance of that!

Richard: Why is your chance any slimmer than the next person's?

Harry: I am not a financial whiz and I haven't worn a business suit in years.

Richard: Are you sure those are the main criteria for being a stockbroker?

Harry: That's the way I always pictured it.

Richard: It's important to find out from a reliable source. Let's ask some stockbrokers about how they got into that profession and what it takes to succeed.

David's draft prototype

Home Address
Date

Name of Addressee
Firm Address

Dear (Name of Addressee):

Would you believe that studying Cicero has helped me prepare for a banking career as a commercial lender? After researching potential careers and identifying my interests, banking is the career I want. Let me tell you how my work experiences and academic studies will help make me an asset for your bank:

Analytical ability: My academic program required analyzing factors influencing historical trends, careful examination of classic texts such as Cicero and rigorous insistence on logical thinking.

Communication: My term papers were evaluated highly for their depth and clarity. Oral exams and presentations were an important part of my program. I assisted co-workers on a summer job in writing letters and memos.

Teamwork: Gained through group projects, team sports, part-time jobs.

Research: I am persistent in digging for facts and meticulous in preparing results.

Judgment: My employers have praised me for using sound judgment, especially in ambiguous circumstances.

Hard worker: Worked 15-20 hours per week during academic semesters, full-time in summer, to finance education.

I am attracted to lending as a career because it would enable me to apply the skills I have already developed while gaining new experiences. My discussions with bankers have led me to conclude that banking is a challenging business that meets a critical need — economic development. Your bank is particularly appealing to me because [. . .].

I hope to meet with you personally to see if there might be a career for me with [name of bank]. Next week I will call you to see if a meeting can be arranged.

Thank you.

Sincerely yours,

David McGrath

David McGrath
Enclosure

Harry knew how to make contacts (see Chapter 11). He prepared a list of questions and met with several stockbrokers. Based on what he learned, Harry came back to see me with some interesting news. "Two of the people I spoke with came into the field after working at something else. Apparently, there are a lot of career changers in that field. None of the people I met was a financial whiz," Harry told me. "From their answers to my questions, I developed a list of positive characteristics needed to succeed as a stockbroker," Harry continued.

I asked Harry if we could look at his list and identify positive characteristics the profession needed that he had. Here is what we discovered:

1. Harry's initial concerns (financial whiz; business suit) seemed unwarranted.
2. Harry possessed many of the key positive characteristics desired in the field.
3. "Sales ability" might seem questionable at first, but Harry did have important pieces of that characteristic.

Seeing the possibility of becoming a stockbroker in a clearer light, Harry sat down and wrote the prototype letter on page 102. His plan was to play out the theme of "hardworking, hands-on businessman wants to apply talents as a stockbroker." Harry inserted brackets to indicate changes he would make in writing to a specific firm.

Harry the Grocer Becomes Harry the Stock Broker

Positive characteristics needed	Positive characteristics I have	Examples
Sales ability	• Persuasion.	• Persuaded suppliers to offer special discounts.
	• Merchandising.	• Arranged aisles and advertising to bring in business.
	• Client base.	• Civic & religious groups; business associations.
Hardworking	• Hardworking.	• 12- to 14-hour days not uncommon.
Gain product knowledge	• Gained product knowledge.	• Mastered relevant facts about 5,000 items in store.
Rejection	• Thick-skinned.	• Deal with abrasive suppliers, finicky customers and staff of mixed quality.
Self-starter	• Self-starter.	• Initiated numerous projects for store; hands-on businessman.

Harry wanted to demonstrate that he was worth interviewing. To achieve that goal, Harry has shown that he has key positive characteristics needed for his intended profession of stockbroker. Harry had learned from his informational meetings that the ability to sell in a generally unstructured environment is a key to success. That's why he focused on hardworking, self-starter characteristics.

But selling was a sticking point. Supermarket merchandising is not sales in the stockbroker sense. Harry finessed the issue in three ways. First, he formatted his letter so that he could highlight positive characteristics in an easily visible way. Second, Harry's supporting examples indicate characteristics important to sales (persuasive ability, attract customer, thick-skinned). Third, Harry indicated a network of possible sales leads he could bring to the job.

Harry also needed to show that he was properly motivated. Notice that he didn't give any negative reason for leaving his current field, only positive ones for desiring stock brokerage. Further, the reason he gave was the main motive for anyone entering that field, namely a chance to earn a substantial income. However, for people interested in most other fields, mentioning money as a motivation would have a negative effect. Harry's reference to that particular firm indicates a connection between his business experience and the firm's clients. If a particular firm's clients are not "small investors," Harry will need to show a connection to the firm through a revised statement.

The closing paragraph reflects Harry's eagerness for a new profession, but no panicked hurry to leave his current one. That's important, because employers are less likely to interview someone who seems to be desperate.

Harry's suggestion for a meeting even if no positions are available is a good one. It reflects a common sales technique of "Let's meet to explore ways." If Harry can arrange to meet even if no openings exist at present, he is ahead of the game if an opening develops in the future.

Bill: engineering some job interviews

Bill was a forthcoming graduate in engineering. The same basic rules apply to Bill as to Jeannette and David, but there is one significant difference: For Bill, technical skills are the single most important positive characteristic to show in his cover letter. He must present them early in the "why you should interview me" paragraph of his letter.

For Bill, the credibility gap (and we all have one) is a function of his future potential. Since the half-life of engineering knowledge is five years or less, Bill needs to show managerial potential. Otherwise, his probability of getting hired in the first place is reduced. Why? Because in five years, if Bill is still just an engineer, his employer may be faced with a relatively well-paid employee who is less current with engineering advances than a recent college graduate. To avoid that dilemma, firms are prone not to hire someone in the first place unless s/he is promotable. Therefore, it is important for Bill to show promotional potential to help obtain an interview at all.

In terms of motivation, Bill's is reflected in part by his choice of majors, but he should try to show a connection to the firm as well.

Keeping these points in mind, Bill produced the prototype letter on page 104. Like others in this chapter, it is written as a generic—that is, specific about the career field, but not directed to a specific company.

Harry's draft prototype

Home Address
Date

Name of Addressee
Firm Address

Dear (Name of Addressee):

My career goal is to be a stockbroker with [name of firm]. Let me tell you what I can offer your firm.

Hard worker: In my current profession, 12- to 14-hour days are not uncommon.

Self-starter: As a hands-on businessman, I plan and execute the tasks we need to be profitable.

Sales ability: I have often persuaded suppliers to offer special discounts to attract customers. I plan everything from aisles to advertising. I am thick-skinned enough to take lumps from suppliers, customers and temporary staff, and I keep on going.

Client base: I have numerous community contacts from my involvement with civic groups, religious organizations and professional associations.

Although I enjoy my current position, I would like to apply my talents to stock brokerage. My main reason for entering this field is the high financial compensation possible for a hardworking producer. [Your firm] is especially appealing to me because of your emphasis on [the type of small investor I have come to know so well].

I hope we can meet even if you have no current openings on your staff. I am in no hurry to make a move, but I could start producing for you on very short notice. On [specific day and date], I will call you to arrange for a meeting.

Sincerely yours,

Harry Granger

Harry Granger

Enclosure: Resume

Bill faced a two-fold challenge. First, he had to show the positive characteristic of technical expertise. Second, Bill had to show that he had managerial potential (leadership, communication) beyond his technical ability. He did well on both points.

If Bill were a graduate of a college highly respected for engineering and/or he was well-above average in academics, he should mention it in the first or second paragraph.

∙∙∙

How much firm-specific research should you do?

If you have a good prototype letter, most of the text can reflect the types of jobs you are seeking and the industry of which the particular firm is a part. These two factors remain constant for all jobs and firms in that industry. The minimum change you need is a sentence stating your motivation for wanting to work for that specific firm. That information could come from promotional literature the firm supplies about itself, the chairman's message in the firm's annual report or an article in the press, for example.

If time permits more extensive research, you could gather material to make your letter even better. You might be able to include positive characteristics such as product knowledge or managerial philosophy, which would link you more clearly with the firm to which you are writing.

In short, the absolutely critical part of your research is about the kind of job you want. Knowledge of the industry is also important, because it would apply to a large number of firms. Firm-specific research could range from the minimum, which would let you write a letter like Anthony's, to a thorough job, which would help you write an outstanding letter like Cecily's.

∙∙∙

A potential weakness for Bill, as with many recent college graduates, is his lack of related work experience. Bill finessed this issue primarily by referring to his hands-on group projects. His reference to employers' praise for his communication skills indicates he has worked. That's as explicit as Bill wanted to get because his college jobs were of the survival variety: waiter, camp counselor and library clerk.

When Bill moves from a prototype to a letter directed to a specific employer, he should individualize his text by referring to the company's products, philosophy, track record, size or geography as being an attraction to him.

Where are we now?

In this chapter, six members of the JSC wrote prototype cover letters. Each person applied general cover letter principles to his or her own situation. Each identified the main points s/he wanted to make before starting to write, a process that makes writing easier and more effective. The comments at the end of each letter should help you review your own text and see if there is room for improvement.

In the next chapter, we will see how to make your cover letter and resume partners for progress.

Bill's draft prototype

Home Address

Date

Addressee Name
Firm Name
Firm Address

Dear (Name of Addressee):

I am interested in joining the engineering department of [name of firm]. The technical expertise I have gained while obtaining my degree in industrial engineering, combined with my work ethic and interpersonal skills, will make me an asset to your firm.

In addition to classroom training in physics, engineering and computers, I excelled in group engineering projects. One of those projects, "Turning Sludge to Silver," gave me hands-on experience in dealing with the kind of challenges your firm faces. But I offer more than technical proficiency. I demonstrated my leadership ability as vice-president of our AIPICS chapter, and my communications skills have been praised by both employers and professors.

My desire for a career in industrial engineering extends back to my pre-college days when I took science and mathematics courses required for entering this major. My attraction to your firm in particular is based on [specific points].

My resume is enclosed. Next week, I will call your office to see if a meeting can be arranged at your convenience.

Sincerely yours,

William Bailey

William Bailey

Enclosure

Quickie letters

Sometimes pragmatic constraints will leave you with two options: A short cover letter or no letter at all. In that case you could use a quickie letter like one of these:

Mr. Tom Jones
Vice President-Administration
Yo-Yo Products, Inc.
3 Bay State Center
Chicopee, MA 01006

Dear Mr. Jones:

My neighbor, Myrna Olde, told me that your assistant at Yo-Yo Products is planning to retire soon. Good people are hard to replace. Could we discuss the possibility that I might be a good successor? I will call you next week to see what you think. In the meantime, my resume is enclosed for your review. Thank you.

Sincerely,

Rose Sostik

Rose Sostik

Enclosure:

Ms. Mindy Stark
General Manager
Stark, Raven & Madd Associates
3563 Walnut Street
Philadelphia, PA 19107

Dear Ms. Stark:

The *Local Ledger* reported that you have just won a government contract to retrain people being downsized in the sardine industry. I have several years of training experience with both blue-collar and white-collar workers. Perhaps I could be an asset to Stark, Raven & Madd Associates as you service this new contract.

My enclosed resume gives more detail about my skills and experience. I will call you next week to see if you think a meeting might be in order.

Sincerely,

Selma Sanchez

Selma Sanchez

Enclosure:

Box 1793
Belchertown Bugle
1500 Huntington Pike
Belchertown, OH 45234

To Whom It May Concern:

The Sunday, May 20, issue of *The Bugle* carried a notice that your firm, described as a leading mousetrap maker, is looking for experienced salespeople. My previous success in selling to both household and industrial customers proves that I have the skills and drive you are seeking. For example, I have been the number-one sales representative in my current territory for three years in a row.

My resume is enclosed. May I look forward to hearing from you soon?

Sincerely yours,

Shirley Ryan

Shirley Ryan

Enclosure:

Chapter 9

....

Your Resume and Cover Letter: Partners in Progress

....

This is a book about *cover* letters. As such, they are letters that cover something, usually a resume. In this chapter, I ask the Job Search Club to write a letter that would be a partner to cover a *specific* resume. That partnership is achieved by making sure that the cover letter adds value to the resume and avoids duplicating it. Your resume is (or should be) a good presentation of your positive characteristics. So how do we avoid duplication? In this chapter, we will see how the JSC achieves this through highlighting, reframing and adding something new, such as motivation.

The Job Search Club was interested in the idea of a partnership between the cover letter and the resume. The JSC asked me to explain the terms I was using and I did, by way of analogy.

The sportscaster's lesson

Many times a sports fan watches a contest that takes two or more hours to complete. Excited, s/he turns on the evening news to hear the sports segment. The thrilling contest that took hours to play is reviewed in a minute or so. Special emphasis is given to the game's highlights: a key base hit, a spectacular catch, a basket at the buzzer, a decisive moment that would interest viewers.

Your resume is something like a TV sports news broadcast: a brief presentation that captures positive characteristics of yours that would interest an employer. Your cover letter can go beyond that. It gives you a chance to *highlight* those positive characteristics that would be of special interest to a *particular* employer. It's as if a TV station could broadcast to your home the highlights of special interest to you, while beaming different highlights to someone who has different interests. What's more, your cover letter can demonstrate motivation. In a sense, your resume can record the play, while your cover letter can add brief comments about the athlete who made it.

The curator's course

Another way your cover letter can be a partner to your resume is through reframing.

Let's think about a museum curator for a moment. The curator might have artifacts from the Aztec civilization. Without distorting the facts at all, s/he could present the artifacts to museum visitors as Aztec, Indian, North American Indian, Pre-Columbian or Mexican, depending upon the interests of the audience. When looking for a job, you can reframe resume items in your cover letter to make them of more immediate interest to your reader.

Dorothy and the Scarecrow

One scene I love in *The Wizard of Oz* is Dorothy's first meeting with the Scarecrow. When Dorothy asks for directions to the Emerald City, the Scarecrow points his arms every possible way. Lacking a sense of direction, the Scarecrow couldn't leave his long-standing place in the cornfield.

Employers avoid people who don't know where they are going. Let the employer know that you have some sense of professional direction by letting him/her know your motivation for following a yellow brick road to that firm.

Harry liked the analogies, but he was interested in seeing some concrete examples. I chose a resume from last year's JSC for this year's members to consider. The JSC members looked at Christopher Stuart Robin's resume (see page 109), and wrote a cover letter as its partner.

After the group had a chance to read Christopher's resume, I asked for ideas on what might be highlighted. This is what the JSC suggested:

Harry: Christopher does seem to be a hard worker. That's certainly an important characteristic.

Gabrielle: He certainly needs to highlight his motivation. He doesn't have any direct retail experience, so motivation has to be especially important to him.

These two points did indeed seem useful. To practice an additional approach, I asked the JSC to identify anything that Christopher might reframe. David suggested that Christopher's experience as a landscaper might be reframed in terms of developing basic business sense. Lauren agreed and added the possibility of using Christopher's experience as an events coordinator to show that he understands what people like.

David then started to draft a cover letter for Christopher, remembering two principles:

1. The cover letter is a partner to the resume. It adds value by highlighting and reframing without duplicating.

2. The cover letter should include new items that didn't appear on the resume at all. Motivation is one example. That's to be expected because the cover letter is directed toward a specific employer or industry.

Christopher Stuart Robin
2210 N. Pleasant Street
Lincoln Heights, NE 68540
(402) 279-1775

SUMMARY: Proven entrepreneurial ability. Demonstrated skills in research, leadership, communication. Seeks position in the retail industry. Developed interest in retail career through running own business and meeting with retail professionals.

EDUCATION: Emeritus College (Railsplit, NE)
Bachelor of Arts, May 1997
Major - History

Self-financed 100% of living expenses and 50% of tuition through academic year and summer jobs.

EXPERIENCE:
1992 - present **Library Assistant/Student Supervisor, Emeritus University**
Demonstrate communication skills by providing research and information services to students and faculty. Maintain circulation records and update daily transactions. Supervise six student workers during evening and weekend hours. Employed 20 hours per week during school terms, full-time during vacation.

Fall 1991 **Proctor, Management Department, Emeritus University**
Led business case analysis for a group of management students. Fostered communication between the professor and students.

Summer 1993, **Entrepreneur - Landscaper**
1992, 1991 Established own business and developed clientele. Maintained lawns and shrubbery for 30 customers (households and businesses). Supervised four employees. Purchased equipment and materials based on quality and probable return on investment. Annual billings averaged $24,000.

Other
employment: **Camp counselor, tennis instructor, lifeguard**

ACTIVITIES **Events Coordinator, Greenough Dormitory Council**
Coordinated fund-raising events; organized social and educational activities for 350 residents.

The draft cover letter David produced is shown on page 111.

Consistent with our usual practice, the JSC members had some questions.

Harry: Is there a basic theme to this letter?

David: Yes, there is: I (Christopher) am a hard worker who is serious about retailing in general and Storeco in particular.

Harry's question and David's response are right on target. Your letter will be much more effective if it conveys a basic theme of interest to the reader. Try summarizing your letter in one sentence and see if you have a succinct theme.

Gabrielle: How did you identify Jennifer Jones?

David: Our general principle is to write to the highest ranking person in the functional area. Storeco's program is designed to produce buyers and Ms. Jones is the senior buyer.

Bill: You are just graduating college. Why not write to the College Relations manager?

David: If they have one, I could. In fact my letter may be referred there. Still, there's no harm in addressing a senior line manager. Her buckslip on top of my letter and resume may even yield some extra attention.

Jeannette: You mention *Fairchild's* under product knowledge. What is that about?

David: *Fairchild's* is a well-known reference directory in the retail industry. I wanted to show that I had learned enough about the industry to utilize this source. Since most job applicants do little if any research, this should be a major point in my favor.

Anthony: Have you considered the possibility that your cover letter and its partner, your resume, might be scanned and stored in a computer's memory?

David: Yes, indeed. I could even use this text for an e-mail, although it would probably take up more space than some templates would permit. Notice that I used different terminology in the two documents. For example, I wrote "entrepreneurial ability" in the resume and "business sense" in the cover letter. In that way, I increase the probability of scoring a computer hit if Storeco searches its job applicant file. I have also specified "Retail Management Training Program," a term Storeco may score as a hit. Mentioning trade publications *(Fairchild's, Retail Weekly)* may also score hits and certainly can't hurt.

Lauren interrupted with a question for me: "Richard, what David is describing is perfectly consistent with a cover letter that will be read and acted upon directly by a human being, isn't it?"

Richard: Yes. Our principle of reframing is consistent with the idea of using synonyms and trade terminology to score hits. Adding something new also fits the scoring hits idea and reframing can't hurt. Our basic principles for cover letters haven't changed because of scanning or computer data storage.

David had done a good job in writing a cover letter to accompany Christopher's resume. Since Christopher was a recent college graduate, I suggested that our next cover letter be written for an experienced worker. Harry volunteered to take on that task. On page 113 is the resume for which Harry would be writing a powerful partner.

Recent college graduate

2210 N. Pleasant Street
Lincoln Heights, NE 68540

October 15, 1996

Ms. Jennifer Jones
Senior Buyer
Storeco, Inc.
5321 Paradise Boulevard
Hope, NE 68543

Dear Ms. Jones:

I am interested in joining Storeco, Inc., through your Retail Management Training Program. My exploration of the retail industry and my research on Storeco have convinced me that this is the best career path for me to follow.

I am certain that the skills and attributes I have developed would help make me an asset to Storeco:

Business sense: I established a profitable landscaping business. This required the ability to address the interests of potential customers and make prudent decisions on pricing.

Hard worker: I supported myself in college through 20 hours of work per week during semesters and full-time work in the summer.

Product knowledge: *Fairchild's* reports that Storeco is the leading footwear retailer in the Midwest. Through research papers and projects, I have gained a good grasp on the shoe business.

Building a career with Storeco would be very appealing to me. First, I want a career where hard work, business sense and product knowledge can lead to success. Second, Storeco managed to maintain impressive growth in a highly competitive environment. As *Retail Weekly* put it, "Storeco has succeeded by correctly anticipating rapid changes in consumer taste and price options." Third, I want to make decisions that will have a direct impact on the bottom line.

My resume is enclosed. Next week, I will call you to arrange for a meeting at your convenience. Thank you.

Sincerely yours,

Christopher Stuart Robin

Christopher Stuart Robin

Enclosure

In his resume, Harry showed that he was the successful manager of a complex, $5-million business. Although his resume already presented some of Harry's positive characteristics, he realized that he could add value to it by:

- Highlighting.
- Reframing.
- Adding something new, like motivation.

Harry sketched a plan (shown below), for his cover letter.

Using this short plan as an outline, Harry wrote the cover letter on page 114 as a partner to his resume.

Harry has drafted a letter that forms a productive partnership with his resume. The first paragraph communicates his purpose in writing and two attributes that should help him be taken seriously (businessman, community contacts). The second paragraph highlights and reframes three characteristics (business sense, persuasion, community ties) that are of particular interest in Harry's prospective career. It also adds a new fact—hard work. This is important in brokerage and was not explicitly stated in Harry's resume.

• •

Theme:
Successful business person with extensive community connections and positive characteristics needed in brokerage.

Opening paragraph:
Quick reference to desire to be a stockbroker.

Second paragraph:
(Why you should interview me.)
Reframe managerial experience to show entrepreneurial aspects. Highlight negotiating ability and community ties.

Third paragraph:
(Why I want to work for you.) Add motivation regarding job (stockbroker) and firm (Jones Marney), for example.

Close: Short, remember to keep responsibility for next step in my court.

• •

The third paragraph provides Harry's motivation, a factor that is extremely difficult to present in a resume. As he had planned, Harry explains his attraction to both the profession and the particular firm to which he is writing.

If Harry is sending his correspondence to a centralized human resource function of a large brokerage firm, his letter and resume are more likely to be scanned. Therefore, Harry could add some buzzwords to increase the likelihood of scoring hits: "Understanding services: I have been reading *NASD* material as a preliminary preparation for my *Series 7* and *Series 63* licenses. I have a solid understanding of how equity and fixed income markets work."

The closing paragraph is appropriately short and indicates that Harry will initiate the next step.

Harry Jordan
1137 Lakeview Drive
Madison, WI 53593
535-555-7893

Summary: Hands-on Manager with record of running a profitable small business. Proven skills negotiating, organizing and supervising.

Experience

Manager: **Value Supermarket, Madison, WI**
Accomplishments: Increased profit margin by 15%. Reduced shrinkage through tighter controls on inventory and enhanced rapport with staff. Expanded customer base utilizing product promotions and free publicity from community service projects. Achieved lowest staff turnover among area supermarkets. Increased revenue sources by $100,000 through negotiated shelf-space premiums. Won Model Business Citizen of the Year Award, 1995.

Responsibilities: Manage $5-million retail super-market. Negotiate shelf-space premiums and advertising fees. Develop annual business plan, including inventory level, product selection and pricing strategy. Hire assistant managers and supervise cash management. Assure friendly service to customers. Track sales of 5,000 different products.

Manager, (1985-present); started as vegetable aisle clerk (1982), rose to assistant manager in 18 months.

Education: Bachelor of Science
Carolina College (Raleigh, NC)

Personal: Active in Civic Affairs: Chairperson, Membership Committee, Bull Moose Lodge. Executive Board, Business Council of Madison. Fund raiser: United Way; Little League.

Harry's cover letter

1137 Lakeview Drive
Madison, WI 53593

April 2, 1997

Mr. Michael Feiner
Vice President
Jones Marney, Inc.
5397 Bourse Boulevard
Madison, WI 53744

Dear Mr. Feiner:

I am interested in joining your firm as a stockbroker. My experience as a successful small businessman and my extensive community contacts should make me an asset to Jones Marney.

Here are some of the attributes that would help me be a successful broker:

Business sense: I took a marginal business and transformed it into the most successful supermarket in our city.

Extensive community ties: As a hands-on manager, I am well-known to our steady customers. In addition, I have numerous contacts with other business people through years of involvement in civic and charitable causes.

Hard work: Seven-day weeks and 12-hour days are not unusual for me.

My interest in stock brokerage stems from two sources. First, I am an avid follower of the financial markets. Second, at this point in my career, the opportunities brokerage provides for income growth are very attractive. Jones Marney is especially appealing to me because of your leadership role in developing investment plans for small businesses.

My resume is enclosed. I am eager to discuss with you personally a possible role for me with Jones Marney. Next week, I will call you to arrange an interview.

Sincerely yours,

Harry Granger

Harry Granger

Enclosure

• •

- Harry mentions "opportunities…for income growth" in his letter. In most cases, you are better off saying nothing about salary or income. The topic of money at this stage is a turn-off to many employers.
- However, being a stockbroker is like being a salesman. In the particular case of sales, a desire for significant earnings is an attraction to employers, rather than a turn-off.
- Could this letter be a prototype for letters to other brokerage firms? Yes, indeed. Harry would need to change only the references to the specific brokerage firm, in this case, Jones Marney.

• •

Some people, like Harry, start by developing a succinct theme and then play it out in the course of their letter. Others, like David, develop a plan on the specifics of what they will highlight, reframe or add. In either case, sketching a short plan before you begin to write will make your letter more effective.

A note about confidentiality and references

One thought to keep in mind while looking for a new job is to keep your current one. For many people, keeping their job search secret is another priority. If you are in that situation, I encourage you to request discretion by indicating that you are writing in confidence:

"I am writing to indicate my interest in exploring a position as a member of your finance staff. Because I am currently employed, I request that you keep this correspondence in the strictest confidence."

Or:

"I am writing to you in the strictest confidence. Recently, I heard at a meeting of the Underwriters Association of greater Boston that you may be looking to add an experienced professional to your staff. Let me tell you a little about what I can bring to your firm."

As a general rule, it is not in your interest to include references with your letter unless they are explicitly requested. That situation is most likely to arise in response to a newspaper ad or a posting on the Web. Your last paragraph could refer to your references in this way:

"As you requested, I have enclosed a list of references. Please let me know if you would like any additional information."

Or:

"The list of references you requested is enclosed. Because of the confidential nature of my job search, please call me before contacting any of them."

If the ad gives only a box number and not a name, I suggest not sending recommendations at all. If the employer will not reveal its name, don't trust it with potentially sensitive information.

Where are we now?

In this chapter, we saw how to write a cover letter that adds value to your resume instead of repeating it. Two extensive examples were given showing how to highlight, reframe and add something new (such as motivation) or an important attribute that is not explicit in your resume.

In the next chapter, we will look at other job-hunt situations where a letter may be useful or necessary.

• • • • • • • • • • • •

Chapter 10

Are All Situations Covered?

Most of this book is devoted to cover letters in an outreach context. Namely, cases in which you have identified a potential employer and want to write to him/her on your own initiative. In some circumstances, a different kind of letter is appropriate. Those letters are the topic of this chapter.

Answering a help-wanted ad

One reason we have emphasized an outreach campaign is that many, perhaps most, jobs are not publicly advertised. Still, newspapers and trade publications are one possible source of employment, so it makes sense to utilize them.

The same principles apply as with outreach letters. However, there is often one advantage for you. The employer will probably describe the positive characteristics of most importance to him/her. That gives you a ready-made agenda for your second paragraph and some hints for your third as well.

Let's take a look at an ancient example to see how a cover letter can be useful even in a most difficult situation.

The Bible relates a story from the time of King Saul. A Philistine giant, Goliath, challenged the Israelites to send a champion against him in a fight to the death. It should come as no surprise that there were no immediate takers. Goliath's height was more than six cubits, his armor weighed 5,000 shekels of brass and the shaft of his spear was "like a weaver's beam."

Now let us imagine that Saul decided to put a help-wanted ad in the newspaper. It might have read like this:

Want ad in the *Bethlehem Post*

ARE YOU PREPARED to risk your life for a good cause? A small but dedicated army seeks a champion to fight the fearsome giant Goliath. The king's own armor and sword are available, if needed. You will be rewarded with the nation's eternal gratitude. Only mighty men of valor need apply. Reply to: King Saul c/o Hillside Camp

For the sake of our story, let's say a shepherd boy named David reads the ad and wants to apply. David is young, small and has never been to war. He is not an obvious candidate. But David knew that if you want something, you go for it. Never turn yourself down for a job by not applying. So he wrote the letter on page 119, trying to maximize his probability of getting an interview.

David's cover letter gained him an interview with a skeptical Saul. The rest is history.

Now let's take a look at a more modern example. Read the following ad carefully and identify the positive characteristics being sought.

Help wanted ad that appeared in *The Salesman*

CAN YOU SELL a $3-million piece of equipment and work like a dog for high commissions? You may be the person we need to take over our eastern territory for x-ray equipment. Proven sales ability a must, knowledge of hospital equipment a plus. Extensive travel required. Qualified applicants only should forward a resume to: Mr. John Vision, Senior Recruiter, Seethru X-Ray, Inc., 1717 Fifth Avenue, New York, NY 10148

Positive characteristics sought

Selling	(proven sales ability a must)
Big-ticket items	($3-million piece of equipment)
Hard work	(work like a dog)
Handle responsibility	(take over eastern territory)
Product knowledge	(knowledge of hospital equipment)
Travel	(travel required)

For the sake of this exercise, I asked Cecily to write a letter from an individual who was currently a nurse but wanted to go into sales.

"If I actually were interested in this position, I would be sunk," Cecily said. "I don't have all the positive characteristics they want."

I told Cecily that if she were interested, she should apply. Although neither the real Cecily nor the fictitious nurse would be an obvious candidate, few people have all the characteristics required for a particular job. Besides, if you want something, go for it. Pursue the lead; let the employer decide whether to invite you to an interview. Further, a well-crafted cover letter can sometimes compensate in part for some characteristics or experiences you may be lacking.

Shepherd's Field
Bethlehem

King Saul
c/o Hillside Camp

Dear King Saul:

I was excited to read in the *Bethlehem Post* that you are seeking a champion. Let me tell you why I am the person you need:

Courage: Killed a lion while guarding my sheep.

Skilled with weapons: Lethal at a hundred paces with my slingshot.

Element of surprise: Because of my size, Goliath won't take me seriously. That will give me the advantage of surprise.

Being your champion is very appealing to me. I have brothers in your army, and I don't want them taken captive. In addition, I am tired of bullies and would like to get this giant off the nation's back. Since I live in nearby Bethlehem, relocating to your encampment poses no problems for me.

It is the wrong century for resumes, but I have enclosed a few ballads about my heroism for your review. Next week, I will contact your tent to arrange a meeting at your convenience.

Sincerely yours,

David Jesseson

David Jesseson

Enclosure:

I asked Cecily to make a Message/Approach chart for this situation, showing what messages she needed to convey and how she would address them. Cecily's chart appears below.

Cecily realized that "Susan Nurse" didn't have everything the ad wanted. On the other hand "Susan" certainly had something to offer. Based on her chart, Cecily drafted the letter on page 121 for "Susan Nurse."

Will a well-conceived text such as the one Cecily wrote guarantee a job interview? Absolutely not. There are never guarantees. Cecily's task is to increase the probability of her being interviewed. A good cover letter will increase the chance of her obtaining an interview, and she really can't expect more than that.

Message	Approach
Positive characteristics	**Indicate**
• Product knowledge.	• Worked in hospital.
• Selling.	• Worked with decision-makers; demonstrated communication skills.
• Hard work.	• Long work days and working weekends are common.
Demonstrate seriousness, professionalism	Research firm thoroughly.
Address doubts: travel, assertiveness.	Willing to travel and work late. Assertive close.

In this case, Cecily decided to put her best foot forward—namely, her experience in a hospital. By emphasizing "Two years' experience" and "Proven ability to deal with decision-makers," she is highlighting two appealing positive characteristics. Cecily also knows that she must deal with the reality of no sales experience as such. Rather than get defensive, Cecily shows that she has gumption by stating "more than sales experience"—namely, a knowledge of how decisions are made. She has handled a potential weakness with compensating strength. That's a good tack to take when you are missing a required positive characteristic.

What to do in the face of rejection

Under the best of circumstances, you will probably receive more rejection letters than invitations to a job interview. Rejections don't have to be seen as final, however. If you remain interested in that firm, there are two approaches you can take following a rejection letter.

1. Write to another manager in the firm. For example, if you received a "no thank-you" from the chief financial officer, you could write to the controller.

2. Send a follow-up letter indicating continued interest.

3322 Maple Lane
Fair Lawn, NJ 07410

February 3, 1997

Mr. John Vision
Senior Recruiter
Seethru X-Ray, Inc.
1717 Fifth Avenue
New York, NY 10148

Dear Mr. Vision:

This is written in response to your notice for a qualified salesperson as out-lined in the January edition of *The Salesman*. I am eager to join Seethru X-Ray in this capacity and I am certain that I will be an asset to your company. Among the qualifications that I can offer to Seethru X-Ray are:

Two years' experience as a manager for a major user of x-ray equipment (Broken Knee Hospital). Intimate familiarity with the use of this equipment and the decision-making process for major purchases.

Proven ability to deal with decision-makers. I meet regularly with the top management of my hospital and participate in determining major policies.

More than sales experience. I know how decisions are made by hospital administrators and how to appeal to their sometimes conflicting objectives.

Excellent communication skills. I am an active member of the Toastmasters Club and speak at many community fund-raising affairs. I have made several presentations to my local chamber of commerce.

The position described in your notice is very appealing to me. It would enable me to combine my interest in sales with my knowledge of your product line. I am particularly attracted to Seethru X-Ray because I know that my growth potential is greatest in a small but aggressive firm. I am quite prepared to travel extensively and to work late to produce sales for Seethru.

My resume is enclosed. I am eager to pursue this matter with you. On February 10, I will contact your office to arrange for a meeting to discuss my qualifications in person.

Sincerely yours,

Susan Nurse

Susan Nurse
Enclosure

On the next page is an example of a follow-up to a rejection letter.

A letter like this takes only a few minutes to write. Although the probability of success is slim, a follow-up letter will enhance your prospects more than no response at all.

A live job lead

Through your networking activities (see Chapter 11), you may discover a job opening that is not advertised in the newspaper or trade publication. It is likely you will hear about such a situation because your acquaintance knows about it from the direct hiring manager.

What an opportunity! A live job lead with a personal referral!

When following up on such an opportunity, always begin your letter by mentioning the individual who informed you of the job, the way the letter on page 124 does. And always be sure to follow up with a thank-you to your contact. Expressing appreciation for such leads is one way to keep them coming.

The job fair

One interesting source of job leads is the job fair. Typically, this refers to a situation where representatives of a large number of firms come together in one place to meet prospective new employees. Sometimes a job fair is sponsored by a single firm that has a large number of openings to fill. In either case, you will have the opportunity to meet one or more potential employers, but probably only for a short period of time. Although your resume will gladly be accepted, the thinking jobseeker doesn't leave things at that. Take a business card from each representative of interest to you and immediately follow through with a letter such as the one on page 126.

Good cover letters should result in obtaining good job interview opportunities. After your interview, I recommend sending a thank-you letter to the person you met. There are two reasons: First, it's the courteous thing to do. And secondly, it's smart. Your thank-you letter demonstrates good business etiquette and communicates your continued interest in the job. Your thank-you letter might look like the one on page 127.

The text is designed to remind the recipient of your meeting, to express continued interest and to recall a part of the interview you feel went especially well.

It is most effective to mail your thank-you letter within a day of your interview. If you interviewed with more than one individual, try to send a short thank-you to each person. Using our principle of modular construction, you could change the sentence that reflects your discussion with the particular individual being addressed. The last sentence might also be changed to "I hope we will have an opportunity to work together."

Some people maintain contact with the interviewer even after their thank-you letter is in the mail. After all, several weeks may pass before the firm decides what step it wants to take next—such as inviting you for another stage of interviews or politely expressing a lack of continued interest. Certainly a phone call seven to 10 days after the interview to express your interest is one possibility. But what about another letter?

....

Follow-up to rejection

1776 John P. Jones Blvd.
Independence, MO 64140

December 12, 1996

Ms. Valerie Belecz
Vice President - Marketing
Gadgetco
1 Rube Goldberg Place
Jefferson City, MO 63043

Dear Ms. Belecz:

Thank you for your letter of December 10. Although I am disappointed that no openings exist at present in your market research department, I certainly understand the reality of the situation.

I remain interested in Gadgetco for the reasons I indicated in my earlier letter. In the hope that an opening may develop in the future, I will contact you periodically to see if the current situation changes.

Sincerely yours,

Robert Brown

Robert Brown

2617 Volunteer Road
Wichita, KS 67208

June 12, 1997

Mr. Ralph Casey
Director of Marketing
Tennessee Toy Company
96 Kefauver Boulevard
Memphis, TN 25702

Dear Mr. Casey:

Last week I was in Memphis and had lunch with a mutual acquaintance, Aaron Victor of Mayhem Toys. We were discussing the status of my job search when Aaron mentioned that you are looking for a good product manager. My six years of experience in a related field—children's designer clothing—could make me the person you need.

My resume indicates a number of my professional accomplishments. However, a personal meeting with you would better indicate if there is a good match between your needs and my talents.

I am eager to explore possibilities with you and I will call you next week to see what you think our next step should be.

Sincerely,

Janice Dagi-Ellis

Janice Dagi-Ellis

cc: Aaron Victor

Enclosure

I suggest writing a follow-up thank-you letter when some job-related event has occurred that you could call to the interviewer's attention, such as the letter on page 128.

A simple, short letter of this type can't hurt you and may go a long way toward helping you. It keeps your name in front of your interviewer without making you seem like a pest.

Accepting or rejecting job offers

The goal of a job search is to obtain one or more job offers. Each offer requires a written response from you.

If you wish to accept a job offer, write a short letter that:

- Refers to the offer letter sent to you.
- Clearly states your acceptance.
- Summarize briefly the terms of the offer.
- Expresses your enthusiasm.

    See the example on page 129.

On the other hand, you may wish to reject a job offer. It is important to do so in a professional manner. Your short letter should include:

- An appreciation for the job offer.
- Nice words about the firm.
- Succinct but pleasant statement of rejection.

Your letter might look like the one on page 130.

As a professional courtesy, you should also call both the firm whose offer you accept and the firm(s) you reject to advise them of your decision.

It makes sense to specify a particular reason for rejecting a job offer when you would have a sincere interest in working for that firm if the impeding circumstance changes. The purpose for specifying your reason for saying no is to leave the door open if circumstances change.

There are several ethical points to remember when writing a letter of this type. Be sincere—don't fabricate a reason. Your reason should not be one you hid during the course of the interview process. And if the reason you are rejecting this job is that you are accepting another, don't try to leave the door open. That would be like accepting an offer of marriage from one individual while stringing along someone else with the other.

Where are we now?

In this chapter, we have seen letters written in response to different situations: a help-wanted advertisement, a job lead from a networking contact, a rejection letter from an employer, a follow-up to a job fair and two possible responses to an offer of employment. The response to a help-wanted ad is much like an outreach cover letter, but you will usually be told some of the positive characteristics the employer is seeking. The response to a rejection letter is based on the premise that your expression of continued interest may help you get another interview, and certainly can't hurt you. The follow-up to a job fair contact allows you to show the initiative and interest that most of your competitors will fail to exhibit.

45 Rom Road
Dorothy, KS 67208

April 18, 1997

Mr. Reynold Nakosteen
Project Manager
Computone
684 Byte Blvd.
Wichita, KS 67208

Dear Mr. Nakosteen:

It was a pleasure meeting you at the Information Systems Career Expo in Hazel Crest yesterday. I enjoyed our conversation about Computone and careers for information systems specialists like me.

Following our discussion, I read the literature you gave me about Computone's product and recent performance. I was impressed and would like to discuss possible job opportunities with you in a quieter environment than a job fair can provide.

Next week, I will call you to see if a meeting can be arranged. I have enclosed another copy of my resume for your review.

Sincerely yours,

Jennifer Brownley

Jennifer Brownley

Enclosure

637 Butterfly Avenue
Amherst, MA 01002

February 14, 1997

Ms. Viola Goodcheer
Director of Marketing
Dreamco, Inc.
3229 Avenue of the Americas
New York, NY 10002

Dear Ms. Goodcheer:

It was a pleasure meeting with you on February 13. I enjoyed our discussion about a position as a marketing assistant with Dreamco, Inc.

I remain deeply interested in a marketing career with Dreamco. In fact, my enthusiasm was increased by our discussion of the snake oil principle, a technique I have utilized successfully for a number of years.

The time and consideration you have given me are very much appreciated. May I look forward to hearing from you about further interviews?

Thank you.

Sincerely,

Jessica Thompson

Jessica Thompson

637 Butterfly Avenue
Amherst, MA 01002

March 1, 1997

Ms. Viola Goodcheer
Director of Marketing
Dreamco, Inc.
3229 Avenue of the Americas
New York, NY 10002

Dear Ms. Goodcheer:

Since our meeting on February 13, I have continued my research about the nocturnal visions industry. It seems that Dreamco has earned top honors in marketing, as the enclosed article from *Hallucination Weekly* indicates. Congratulations!

Sincerely,

Jessica Thompson

Jessica Thompson

97 West St.
Amherst, MA 01002

March 26, 1997

Ms. Lauren LaDuc
Director of Operations
Harbor Harmonics, Inc.
7973 Beacon St.
Lexington, MA 02173

Dear Ms. LaDuc:

Thank you for your letter of March 5 in which you offered me employment as a field analyst with Harbor Harmonics. I am excited about your offer and I am glad to accept it.

To review the essence of our agreement, I am to start work in the Boston office on Monday, July 5, with an annual compensation of $45,000 plus fringe benefits.

I look forward to starting work with Harbor Harmonics and to making a solid contribution from the very beginning.

Enclosed is the Employee Data Form that you requested.

Sincerely yours,

Carolyn Krzystofik

Carolyn Krzystofik

Enclosure

97 West St.
Amherst, MA 01002

March 27, 1997

Mr. Robert Asebrook
Vice President - Finance
Bay Brick, Inc.
1515 North Shore Rd.
Brockton, MA 02146

Dear Mr. Asebrook:

Thank you for your letter of March 1 in which you offered me a field analyst position with Bay Brick, Inc.

I was excited to hear from you, in part because of my positive experiences in meeting with you and the members of your staff. However, after considerable thought, I have decided to accept an offer from another firm. I believe this decision is in the best interests of my career at this time.

Your time and consideration are deeply appreciated. I hope that our paths will cross again, perhaps at a meeting of the Financial Fitness Association.

Sincerely yours,

Carolyn Krzystofik

Carolyn Krzystofik

Chapter 11

••

Networking: What It Is, How to Use It

••

There's an old saying: "It's like having an uncle in the carpet business." That is, if you are well-connected, you can get what you want more easily or on better terms. Wouldn't it be great to have an uncle or aunt in the hiring business?

In fact, being connected to an uncle/aunt, colleague, neighbor or whomever is one of the most effective ways people find employment.

Here is what an individual may be able to do for you:

- Give you information about a career, an industry or a particular firm. Knowledge is empowerment and a professional doing the work you would like to do can be an incredible source of information and insights you wouldn't get from a book.

- Give you references to more "uncles/aunts" so your circle of contacts can expand.

- Give you leads to specific job openings (sometimes).

Let's start our look at networking from the worst plausible assumption: You just don't have an "uncle/aunt" in the career field of interest to you. Don't worry. For career purposes, you can develop an extended family. The Job Search Club discussed this topic at one of its meetings. Let's play out the story as David experienced it.

David was concerned that he wouldn't know where to start. He was interested in financial analysis but didn't know a soul in the field. I suggested to David that we could create contacts where none yet existed, and the best place to start was with his immediate relatives and close neighbors. These people will always talk to you just because they know you. David made a chart like the one on page 132 showing his family members and neighbors, along with their respective professions. We called these his "warm contacts."

David's relatives and close neighbors
(warm contacts)

Relatives:

Immediate Family:

Mother: lawyer

Father: sales—computers

Stepfather: beverage distributor

Sister: Still in high school

Brother: joined a hermit club;
   he'll have to work someday

Aunts:

Deliliah: owns beauty salon

Myrtle: computer specialist

Uncles:

Sam: government employee

Mike: professional wrestler

Cousins:

Jean: unemployed

Ollie: makes bullet-proof vests

Bernie: market researcher

Neighbors:

Lon: retired; was in customer service

Alyse: environmental adviser

Ted: public accountant

Mindy: nurse

Friends:

Rip: hasn't awakened to the fact that
   he even needs a job.

Morgan: worked for a bank last
   summer

Suzette: just graduated, works in
   public relations

At first glance, David is still in a bind. None of his warm contacts are financial analysts. But he looked at the list more closely and identified a number of people who might be able to help.

Father: Maybe some of his clients are involved with financial analysis.

Delilah: Some of her customers could be financial analysts.

Ollie: Does he have at least one financial analyst in his bullet-proof vest company?

Morgan: I haven't been interested in banking, but maybe I should check out credit analysis and lending.

Ted: Many public accountants leave their firms to work for clients. Some of them go into financial analysis. Maybe some of Ted's old friends could help.

Alyse: I hadn't thought about a nonprofit or advocacy group. However, with all the discussion about reconciling environmental goals and business interests, there might be a role there for me.

These six people seemed to be the most likely sources of help to David. David would arrange to meet with each of them. If time permitted, David would speak to everyone on his warm contact chart including Lon (retired) and Jean (unemployed). You never know who people know.

Although none of David's warm contacts were financial analysts, we saw that a number of people close to David could help him connect with people who were. This second circle of potential "uncles/aunts," the associates of relatives, the friends of neighbors (or even the neighbors of friends) we called "tepid contacts."

After speaking with his warm contacts, David found that most would be willing to put him in touch with financial analysts they knew. The exception was his mother, who felt she couldn't mix client business with a family interest. That's a professional reality and David understood it as such. For his part, David sent each tepid contact a short letter such as the one on page 134.

A letter such as David's isn't absolutely necessary in this case, since John Giraldi already expected to hear from David. Still, it is a good idea to write, because it lends a professional air to David's subsequent meeting with John.

Before David called John, we discussed any concerns David might have.

David: Why should John Giraldi agree to see me? A friend of mine wrote him last month about a job interview and received a negative response.

Richard: John will be willing to see you for two reasons. First, you are Myrtle's nephew and he doesn't want to offend a co-worker (or possibly his superior) by saying no. Second, conducting a job interview is relatively expensive in terms of time and may carry with it some legal baggage as well. An informational meeting doesn't carry with it either legal baggage or commitments of any kind. It can also be kept short.

David: Okay, but what will I gain from my meeting? I have read everything ever written about financial analysis.

Richard: I am not sure anybody has really read everything there is to read about anything, but let's assume you are right. Faces are friendlier than paper. A real person can tell you about his or her own experiences and insights. You will also be able to ask about your own concerns and get a practitioner's point of view. In short, a person in a profession can give you insights and information that are not written anywhere and give it to you with a human dimension.

David: Fine, but let me push this a little further. What practical good will that information be for a cover letter, let's say?

Richard: If you are better informed about the three key areas (career, firm, industry; see Chapter 2), you can write a more compelling cover letter. That means more job interviews. There is something else. The very fact that you have been speaking with professionals about a desired career will help show how well-motivated you are—and that will make you more attractive to employers.

1357 Samson St.
Goshen, MA 01032

September 10, 1996

Mr. John Giraldi
Senior Financial Analyst
Clip-On, Inc.
Enfield, CT 06083

Dear Mr. Giraldi:

I am writing to you at the suggestion of my aunt, Myrtle Spruce, who works for your firm. Myrtle knows of my interest in becoming a financial analyst when I graduate from college in May. She suggested that you might be a good person to speak with to learn more about the profession.

If you could meet with me for 15 to 30 minutes, your experiences and insights would help me enormously. Let me assure you that I am seeking your advice, not a job interview.

I will call you next week to see if a brief meeting can be arranged.

Sincerely,

David McGrath

David McGrath

David: Information and insights are fine, but why not ask directly for a job lead?

Richard: You need to be careful about this. There are two reasons. First, the meeting was arranged on the basis of "I'm looking for information." It's unethical to change the stated purpose of the meeting when you are in someone's office, just as "bait-and-switch" techniques are unethical in advertising.

Second, it would be neither wise nor necessary. It's not wise because the professional with whom you are meeting may be offended by the agenda change. It's also unnecessary. If you present yourself well (you are thoroughly prepared; you ask good questions), the professional will be as helpful as he or she can be. That may well include referrals or job leads.

David: Does that mean you couldn't ask for a job lead at all?

Richard: No, it doesn't. But be careful not to stray from your stated purpose—information. You could ask, for example, "How would a person soon to graduate college enter this profession?" or "Does this profession tend to be in high demand? If so, in what kind of industry?"

I wouldn't ask, "Are there any openings in your department?" If there are, and if you have presented yourself well, the professional will probably volunteer the information. In addition, you are going to ask for leads for more informational meetings. Increase the chance of getting a "yes" to that request by avoiding the complications that "Do you have a job for me?" can bring with it.

David was almost convinced. "I'm ready to start meeting with my tepid contacts," he said. "Not quite yet," I replied.

Be prepared

Like many people, David hadn't yet thought about his anticipated meeting with John Giraldi. Of course, he was going to put on a suit ("I don't want to look out of place"). However, David needed to realize that he should prepare for an informational meeting as thoroughly as he would for a job interview. There are two good reasons.

First, preparation is essential if your questions are going to yield useful answers. Second, you want to impress the professional with whom you are meeting with the idea that you might be a success in the field. That will make him/her more likely to extend an effort to help you. Coming prepared suggests that you would be prepared for your professional meetings. Being unprepared suggests the opposite.

At my urging, David took the following steps to prepare for his informational meeting. First, he did some research on financial analysis as a career using the sources we discussed earlier. Second, David read materials about Clip-On and the office supply industry (see Chapter 2). Third, he visited his local office supply store to see how Clip-On products were being merchandised. Fourth, David tried to visit a place where Clip-On products were used to inquire about a consumer viewpoint. It's a good idea to get a feel for a firm's products in use or at least in a store.

Now that he was prepared, David could go to his meeting with John Giraldi and benefit from it. He arrived at Clip-On 15 minutes before his appointment time. "You can't be late if you are early," David reasoned. John came to pick up David from Clip-On's waiting area and they spent a few moments just chatting. John wanted it that way so they both would feel more at ease. David realized that the initiative for getting down to business lay with him, so he made the transition from the small talk to the matter at hand:

David: I appreciate your agreeing to speak with me this morning. I know how important your time is, so we'll make it a point to keep our meeting within the 15 to 30 minutes I mentioned when I called.

I have been investigating careers in financial analysis and I would appreciate your advice. So far, my research has been confined to books. I am hoping to gain a better picture by meeting with professionals like you. I have prepared a number of questions. Would you mind if I took notes?

John was impressed when he heard that David had come to the meeting prepared. He felt pleased to share his experiences with David. The table on page 137 indicates the kind of questions David prepared to ask at informational meetings. When he met with John, these questions were amended a bit to reflect a more direct bearing on Clip-On.

After the meeting, David wrote John a brief thank-you note and called his Aunt Myrtle to thank her, too. But what did David learn from his meeting? There are two parts to that question: First, what John said; second, how David processed the information. David reviewed what he had learned and made the chart on page 139 to summarize the situation and compare his work values with those he perceived in John. There were bound to be both differences and similarities.

David realized from reviewing his chart that even a cerebral job like financial analysis involved a good deal of interpersonal skill. Further, it seemed as if some skill in subjective judgment is involved. "You can't depend on a computer to give you all the answers," John had told him.

Fortunately, John was impressed by David's preparation and the way he presented himself. When David asked for some additional contacts for informational meetings, John was able to suggest a few names. David did not ask directly about job leads. However, John volunteered the fact that he was unaware of any current hiring plans at Clip-On but, "I will let you know if anything develops." David made a note to contact John periodically to check on the possibility of new job leads. In the meantime, David continued with his informational interviewing.

Courtesy is a valuable interpersonal attribute and it applies to networking. After each informational interview, I would immediately send a brief thank-you note, which should express appreciation for time and assistance, an example of some way in which you benefited from the meeting and a reference to staying in touch.

Your thank-you letter might look like the one on page 140.

Cold calls

David had followed his warm contacts to tepid contacts who were in the profession of interest to him. Typical of job-seekers, his meeting with John Giraldi was not the only one he arranged. Still, David remembered my suggestion that he should cast his net even wider. When he was prepared to reach out to cold contacts, he and I discussed his next step.

David: I am learning a lot from my tepid contacts. Why bother with cold contacts? That seems like more work with an uncertain payoff.

Richard: There are several advantages to expanding your network:

- More contacts mean more insight from professionals and a greater possibility of job leads.
- Sometimes tepid contacts can fall into a limited set of industries or firm sizes. You want to get the most varied exposure possible.

What did David ask?

The questions David brought with him might provide some useful ideas for you:

What is the job like?

1. What are some of the things you like best about your job? How about things you like the least?
2. Is there such a thing as a typical day or week, and could you describe it?
3. Why is your position important to the firm?
4. Is most of your work done as an individual or as part of a team?
5. Do you still find your job challenging? Why?
6. How do you keep current with the field? Are there professional journals you read regularly?
7. To what extent are technological advances such as new computers or software used on your job?

Career path

1. I would love to know what first brought you into this field. Can you tell me how your career got started? Is this how newcomers get started today?
2. What skills or personal attributes does it take to succeed in this profession?
3. Have there been any particular events that proved to be turning points in your career?
4. With 20/20 hindsight, is there anything you could have done differently that would have made your career more satisfying personally or more rapidly developing professionally?
5. If a relative of yours said to you "I am considering going into this field," what would you say to him/her?
6. How do you think this profession might evolve over the next 10 years or so?
7. Do you belong to any professional societies? Would a nonmember be able to attend a meeting?

Your job, your life and the world outside

1. How do you manage to balance the demands of your work life with the demands of your personal life?
2. Could you tell me about factors outside this company that have an impact on your professional life? For example, the economy, government regulations, competing firms?

The next step

1. You have been very helpful to me. [If possible, give a few examples of what you have gained from the meeting.] Could you suggest the name of one or two other professionals you know who might be helpful to me? I am planning to continue my exploration into this field.

- The process of trying to arrange cold contacts is good practice for an outreach campaign.

David: I see the advantage, but how would I go about it?

Richard: Let's identify sources:

- Firms within commuting radius to your residence or your college.
- Membership lists from professional associations. Your tepid contacts in the field may be willing to share their membership lists with you. If not, check the *Encyclopedia of Associations* to find the association's home office. They may be able to help you.
- Join a professional association that will plug you into a discussion of the latest issues, help show your seriousness and give you a membership list of your own. These people can then be approached for information based on a common bond. A typical fee for a professional association is $30 to $50. This is a small investment that can pay major dividends.

David: Should I just call my prospective cold contacts?

Richard: It's much better to write a letter first. Your letter will increase the possibility of getting a "Yes, I'll meet with you" response when you telephone.

David proceeded to write a cold contact letter like the one on page 141.

Been around the block before

Lauren had been listening closely to David's story. After years of work experience, would Lauren follow the same process as David, a recent college grad? This is what I suggested to Lauren:

When you are looking for a job, it generally makes sense to utilize all the resources that are potentially available to you. (I said "generally" because if you need to keep your search a secret from your current employer, you would need to be more careful.) On that basis, utilizing your warm connections and your tepid connections still makes sense.

Lauren's great advantage is that she already has a large number of potential networking contacts based on her co-workers, customers, suppliers and counterparts in other organizations. She may even have the financial resources to suggest a lunch meeting with a contact. The less formal environment of a meal may make conversation easier. In addition, the meeting will extend beyond the 15 to 30 minutes David would be scheduling.

Terra incognito

Harry raised an interesting point: "I am somewhere in between. Although I have been working for a number of years, I am planning to change careers, not just employers. Would my situation be different from David's or Lauren's?"

I suggested that the principles would remain the same. In terms of specific applications, Harry could benefit from joining a professional association in his anticipated new field. (David also needed to do this; Lauren probably held memberships already.) Harry needed to learn about a whole new field, Lauren needed to learn

....

Gaining a perspective on financial analysis

What John told David	John's perspective	David's perspective
Challenged intellectual abilities, especially re: analyzing cause, change.	Glad to have it, but not a top priority.	I want an intellectual challenge.
Important to ask good questions of people and of the data.	Easier to ask the data than the people.	My interpersonal skills are strong. That might compensate for my good, but not excellent statistical skills.
Financial analysts are accepted but not honored at Clip-On; this firm gives highest prestige to product development people.	Sometimes an aggravation. Product managers sometimes see financial concerns as an impediment to their creative genius.	I really need to keep my mind on how similar jobs can feel different in dissimilar circumstances.
Stress caused by tight deadlines and incomplete information.	It's a good character-builder. It comes with the territory.	I always met deadlines in college, but I had longer lead-times. Could I stand the acid indigestion the stress would cause me?
The intra-office politics can be intense; everyone wants to be CFO. On the other hand, we are a friendly group; some real social ties made.	John wants to be CFO; says he will play the game.	I'm a competitive person, but I'm not as ambitious as John. Assuming I could do the work, could I also play the game? On the other hand, I am glad that there is a sense of social camaraderie there.

....

David McGrath
1357 Samson Street
Goshen, MA 01032

September 21, 1996

Mr. John Giraldi
Senior Financial Analyst
Clip-On, Inc.
Enfield, CT 06083

Dear John:

Thank you for meeting with me on September 20. Your insights and advice about a career as a financial analyst shed some important light on this field. Of particular interest to me was learning about your forecasting activities in conjunction with the marketing department. I hadn't realized the extent to which presentation skills and subjective judgments played a role in your profession.

I am continuing to explore a career in financial analysis. Thank you for giving me the name of Sheila Frankel at Computerco. I am meeting with Sheila next week. As we discussed, I will let you know how my career plans unfold.

Sincerely,

David McGrath

David McGrath

A letter to a prospective cold contact

76 Prospect Street
St. Paul, MN 54144

October 19, 1996

Ms. Dorothy Pokros
Senior Financial Analyst
Heavyduty Manufacturing Co.
17 Nuts & Bolts Drive
Iowa City, IA 52333

Dear Ms. Pokros:

As a fellow member of the Financial Analysts Society, I am interested in seeking your advice. I will be graduating in May 1997, from Emeritus College and I have been meeting with professionals like you to learn more about careers as a financial analyst. To date, I have learned a great deal. However, none of the analysts I spoke to worked in a manufacturing environment.

I am increasingly convinced that a career in financial analysis is what I want, but I'm not sure what kind of work environment would be best. I would appreciate about 15 to 30 minutes of your time to give me some insights in that regard. Next week, I will call you to see if a brief meeting can be arranged.

I assure you, Ms. Jones, that I am seeking information, not a job interview.

Sincerely,

David McGrath

David McGrath

about new employers and a larger role in her current field. Both would benefit from speaking with professionals in their new work environments.

A note before calling

In those cases where Harry or Lauren want to contact someone they don't already know, a brief letter sent before telephoning is in order. The letter's basic format would be much like David's. However, a few changes would be helpful.

For Lauren: She should indicate, "I am exploring possible next steps in my career development" in her initial paragraph. Her middle paragraph, which tells a little about her background, should indicate her experience without sounding like a sales pitch. For example, "By way of background, I have been working as a marketing professional with a medium-sized manufacturer for about five years. After mastering the fundamentals and learning about policy-making issues, I am interested in moving to a higher level of responsibility."

Lauren doesn't need to mention her current firm by name if she is concerned about potential repercussions with her current employer.

For Harry: A statement such as "I am exploring ways to apply my skills to a new endeavor" should appear in his initial paragraph. The middle paragraph might say, "Let me tell you a little about my work history. I have held responsible positions in marketing for a number of years and have been commended by my employers for my contributions. As I look forward to the second half of my career, I would like to find a way to combine my analytical and creative skills in a new field. Opportunities to do that with my current employer seem limited in the present economic climate, so I am weighing the possibility of moving on."

A note of caution

Neither David nor Lauren (nor you) should expect that every tepid or warm contact will agree to see you. However, continue to pursue your networking even if only one in five of your potential contacts agrees to meet with you. The information (and possible job leads) you acquire will be incredibly helpful.

Where are we now?

In this chapter you have seen how to establish a network of professionals who can help you in your job search—even if you need to start from scratch. You learned that it is necessary to be as prepared for an informational interview as for a job interview. I suggested a number of questions you could ask and reminded you to think about what you hear, rather than accepting it as revealed truth.

In the next chapter, we will work on a broadcast strategy.

Chapter 12

•••

Finding
Job Leads

•••

So far, we have seen how the Job Search Club learned to write a good cover letter and how to amend a prototype letter so that it could be sent to many potential employers. But how is it possible to identify those employers? That is the topic of this chapter.

A garden or a wasteland?

Gabrielle volunteered for the task of identifying potential employers. Remembering the research other JSC members had done before writing their cover letters (Chapter 2), Gabrielle decided that she, too, would start in the reference section of her library. The reference librarian helped Gabrielle identify this reference as a helpful source:

Million Dollar Directory
Dun & Bradstreet

There were three volumes in the set. "These would be good for my weight-training class," Gabrielle said as she measured their heft. "I wonder if I will be able to figure out how to use them."

Gabrielle realized that she needed to get an overview of what these volumes contained and how they were organized. She noted that the *Million Dollar Directory* had three criteria for inclusion. A firm must have:

- 250 or more employees at that location.
- $25 million or more in sales volume.
- Tangible net worth greater than $500,000.

Gabrielle made a note to find out the meaning of "tangible net worth" and then she whistled through her teeth: "There are over 160,000 companies listed in this directory, and that doesn't include businesses like my Aunt Dot's print shop, which has 100 employees."

With a combination of awe and concern Gabrielle considered her next step. "I've got to find an organizing principle for this material," she said to herself. Luckily, the directory itself had considered the question. The firms listed were cross-referenced in two indexes. The first was a cross-reference by geography, the second was a cross-reference by industry. Gabrielle saw that both indexes used something called an "SIC code." She learned that the SIC code grouped certain industries together and assigned each grouping a four-digit code number. For example, department stores are 5311; branches and agencies of foreign banks are 6081; bottled and canned soft drinks and carbonated waters are 2086.

Thinking it through, Gabrielle realized that the sheer number of firms included in the directory was an asset, not an obstacle. "Let's say I want to live in Dallas, Texas," Gabrielle thought to herself. "The geographic index will tell me all the firms in Dallas that meet the directory's inclusion criteria. If only a few industries are of interest to me, I can pare down the list by pulling only the relevant SIC codes."

"If a particular industry is my primary concern, I can use the industry cross-reference index," Gabrielle continued. "That's organized by SIC code first, and then by states within each code number. So if I wanted to identify department stores, for example, I could look under SIC code 5311. I could quickly include only those states of serious interest to me."

"Both cross-references give me the page number in the main part of the directory. I'll use each cross-reference to identify firms in the category I want. Then I will look in the main pages to get the information I need about each particular firm," Gabrielle concluded.

Gabrielle decided to use department stores in Dallas as an example of identifying employers. She looked in the geographical index under Dallas, and then followed the sequence of SIC codes to 5311. Gabrielle noted the names of six department stores and the page number where information about each store could be found. Sitting a thousand miles away, Gabrielle was starting to build a list of potential employers where she wanted to live (Dallas) in a field of interest to her (retail).

Gabrielle reasoned that if there is one reference on a subject, there are probably others as well. Sure enough, it didn't take long for Gabrielle to find:

The Career Guide 1997
Dun's Employment Opportunities Directory
Dun & Bradstreet

"I wonder how this book is organized and if it's any different than the *Million Dollar Directory*," Gabrielle said as she read the preface pages. "After all, they come from the same publisher."

The first thing Gabrielle noted was that *"The Career Guide* is designed to ease the job search...." This volume is more directly related to our JSC's immediate needs, Gabrielle realized. But what are the qualifications for listing? Originally, "only those leading U.S. companies having at least 1,000 employees" were included. *The Career Guide* should be easier to use, Gabrielle realized, in part because it would include fewer firms than the *Million Dollar Directory*. Gabrielle read that *The Career Guide* material was also cross-referenced by geography and industry and included nonprofit employers. "At this point, I need to learn how to use a directory to identify potential employers. I will do some work in each directory so I can become familiar with them both."

"Let me change the example a bit. Let's say I am planning to live in Boston and that my career interest is in sales," Gabrielle thought to herself. "Why don't I explore firms there?" Gabrielle opened the cross-reference indexes to see what they provided her. There were 48 listings for sales under Boston. Each contained:

- Firm name address.
- Reference to page number in white pages.
- SIC Code(s).
- Disciplines hired: a list of college majors in which the firm might have interest.

Going down the listing, Gabrielle found several firms that listed her old college major, math, as being of interest. "I guess I'll make note of those and skip the rest," Gabrielle said to herself.

Gabrielle's glitch

Gabrielle may be doing herself a disservice here. "You are who you are," not "you are what you studied." It is usually better to use directory information in a broad, inclusive way and not eliminate a firm from consideration simply because your college major isn't mentioned in connection with that firm. What you have to offer a firm is broader than just the subjects you have studied.

Looking at the citations in the main pages, Gabrielle found a brief snapshot of each firm. The text gave information about "disciplines hired," a company overview and a few sentences about career opportunities.

Some of the firms seemed to be of interest to Gabrielle, based on their product—for example, computers. On the other hand, others were of less interest to her, such as hospitals. "When I make my reports at the JSC meeting, I will ask what to include or exclude when building a list of firms. Maybe there's a rule of thumb about establishing priorities," Gabrielle said to herself.

Gabrielle realized that there's more to Massachusetts than Boston. So she identified firms located in towns a commutable distance from that city. In so doing, she added about 150 firms to her list.

"I've done pretty well in the yellow index," Gabrielle said to herself. "Let's see what else I can find." Gabrielle came to the green index, "Employer Branch Offices Geographically." Under Boston alone, Gabrielle found hundreds of firms having headquarters elsewhere, but branches in Boston. "I will have to dig a little deeper to find addresses and similar information for these branches, since that is not included in the directory. But the important thing is that I have made an important discovery in about one hour of work. Far from having to look for work in a job desert, I really need to identify the most promising roses in a large garden of employers."

Gabrielle's rule of thumb for priorities

Gabrielle left two questions open for herself. Let's address them here:

Priorities: Is there a rule of thumb to identify those firms to which you will devote the most effort? Although every individual has his/her own circumstances, I recommend starting with firms meeting at least two of your most important criteria. For example, you might choose your most desired geography and most desired industry. Then loosen the constraints a bit on one criterion at a time. You could expand your geographical boundaries, for example. That way, you will have a manageable, but growing list of potential employers.

Information about branches: Remember that basic information about the firm's product line, gross revenue, etc., is included in the main entry of the reference books Gabrielle used. If you are interested in a branch location, rather than the headquarters, what you still need to know is its size, address and a contact person. The chamber of commerce in that locality may be able to provide the information. If not, call the branch and simply ask for the name of the senior official. The local telephone book should provide both an address and a phone number.

Small can be beautiful

Gabrielle had discovered ways to identify firms with a large number of employees. Our next step was to have the JSC explore the growing job market in small firms. Looking into small firms may strike some people as unappealing. An image of the low-skill, low-pay, low-prestige job seems to persist despite significant evidence to the contrary. Some people still limit themselves to large firms with well-known names, even though many of these companies are downsizing.

The Job Search Club will look into this perception problem. Then we will learn how to access this growing but hard to identify market.

Why famous is fashionable

Some of the Job Search Club members were discussing their outreach strategy. "I am going to focus on the Fortune 500," Jeannette said. "I want to play ball in the big leagues." Bill had a similar view, but with a different reason. "After busting my tail to do well in college, I don't plan to tell my friends that I work for Mom & Pop Enterprises. I deserve better." Lauren seemed to agree. "We have emphasized the value of research. It has to be easier to identify and research large firms than small firms. Mom & Pop Enterprises may not even publish an annual report."

I listened carefully to what the JSC members were saying. Given my job as a career professional, I accept everyone's feelings about a job situation without passing judgment. However, it is also important that people base their feelings on accurate information. Here are some of the ideas I shared with the JSC to help them see a fuller picture of the big employer/small employer reality:

The value of prestige: There may well be more prestige in working for a well-known firm, and well-known usually means large. But once you start working, the substance of your job and your working environment will be the critical factors. The value of prestige tends to pale by comparison. Big is better-known, but not necessarily better for you.

Compensation: Big salaries go with big companies at the top of the ladder, but not necessarily on the first rung. Sometimes we read about a senior executive of a large firm making millions of dollars in compensation. But how many seven-figure salaries are there and what would it cost you in terms of your lifestyle to get there? Overall, compensation packages for the typical employee vary among big businesses as well as small. Generalizing based on firm size may be a major mistake.

Mobility: There has long been a feeling that having the name of a well-known employer on your resume would be an asset in moving to a new job. This was often true, partly because every large firm had a corporate bureaucracy with jobs similar to those in other firms.

Whatever its previous merit, this idea is probably less valid today. Large employers are downsizing in general and cutting corporate bureaucracies in particular. Big corporations are reorganizing into smaller, more directly accountable business units that are beginning to resemble small businesses.

Today, successful experience with a small firm may lead to broader responsibilities and greater job mobility than being a corporate bureaucrat for a large firm.

Big market in small firms

Lauren asked me what is meant by "small business" and "large business" and how much job growth has there actually been. This is a summary of what I told her:

- Generally, a firm with 500 or more employees is considered to be a "big" business. Since about 15,000 U.S. firms meet that definition, "big" obviously includes more than the Fortune 500. A business employing 25,000 or more people we might call "very big."

- "Small" business is often broken into three statistical categories we could think of in this way:

  > Very small:
  > 1 to 19 employees
  >
  > Medium small:
  > 20 to 99 employees
  >
  > Large small:
  > 100 to 499 employees

Growth v. downsizing. *Business Week* reported these startling facts:

- Very small firms accounted for 57 percent of expected job growth in 1993 (that's 57 percent of 2.1 million jobs).

- An additional 23 percent of the expected job growth was accounted for by medium small firms.

- Three times as many very big businesses anticipated layoffs as anticipated adding jobs.

- Between 1987 and 1991, there was a decrease of 2.4 million jobs in big businesses. In the same period, employment rose by 4.4 million in very small businesses and by 1.4 million more in medium small businesses.

Anthony asked the next logical question: "We learned how to access big business from Gabrielle's experience," he said, "but what sources can we use to identify and then research small business?"

I suggested to Anthony three good sources: chambers of commerce, trade associations and articles in the local press.

Chambers of commerce

Across the United States there are hundreds of local business organizations carrying the name "chamber of commerce." These chambers exist for the purpose of fostering business, and you can find them even in relatively small towns.

Let's say you wanted to explore employment opportunities in the town of Chicopee, Massachusetts (population 55,000). The Chicopee Chamber of Commerce will provide job-seekers access to a reference book identifying 900 employers in the area! The reference is easy to use, indicating the size and line of business of each employer. A very few will be large firms, like Spalding Sports Worldwide. Many will be so small, such as "Joe's Luncheonette," that you will see scant opportunity there.

Most firms will be smaller than Spalding and larger than Joe's. The problem then is to cut down 900 employers to a workable size. You can do this by establishing two criteria for your first group of firms. Manufacturers with more than 20 employees would be an example. An added bonus of this method is that it makes writing your prototype cover letter easier. All your letters for this group will have your professional field, the firm's industry and the matter of location in common. Only one sentence, a motivation for wanting to work for that specific company, would need to be changed for each letter.

Trade associations

The membership list of the local chapter of a trade association provides a useful source of names for networking. These lists also indicate, at least potentially, firms that hire people in your field.

Most professions have at least one association of members who have banded together to protect and promote their interests. A good source for identifying trade associations is:

The Encyclopedia of Associations
Gale Research Co.

This is a readily available reference identifying the purpose and main address of thousands of organizations. A simple inquiry to the group's main office should lead you to the local chapter of that association. Trade associations are good sources for information about current conditions in the profession. Although trade associations vary in their scope and helpfulness, they represent a resource you don't want to overlook.

Trade associations are also a useful source for networking, a topic we discussed in Chapter 11.

Articles in the press

The print media are an outstanding source of stories about firms, business leaders and business conditions. Here are some examples:

- **Local newspapers.** The local press often runs stories about new businesses, expansions (or closings) and prominent local business people. Such stories are a good source for identifying companies of interest. In addition, your cover letter can cite information you read and be addressed to someone mentioned in the article.

You could even open your letter with a bit of subtle flattery like this:

• •

"The recent story in the *Belchertown Bugle* about growing firms grabbed my attention. I was particularly struck by your insight that '. . . it is possible to make a dollar in a recession if you think ahead and work with a passion.' Forward thinking and a passionate commitment to my work have characterized my career. Perhaps we could meet to explore ways in which I could be an asset to you as you build Dreckco into 'a giant in its niche.'"

• •

• **Business press.** Magazines such as *Inc.* report on growing small businesses. In some issues, lists of firms that are the "fastest" something or "potentially most" something are given. Less well-known are regional business publications that cover small business and area economic conditions. Check with your local library or chamber of commerce for the names of specific publications of this kind that might be available to you.

Computer bulletin boards

One aspect of using the computer in your job search is job openings posted on computer bulletin boards. There are numerous bulletin boards, some of which are geographically or functionally specific. Most are available at no charge to the job seeker. A list of some prominent bulletin boards will be found at the end of this section.

In terms of your cover letter, how does that change things for you? It depends upon how you are asked to reply.

By conventional mail. To use our baseball analogy, we're still playing on grass. It is no different than replying to a help-wanted ad in a newspaper. There is an advantage to you in that the job posting may be more current because electronic bulletin boards can be changed faster than newspapers.

By e-mail. The substance of your cover letter doesn't need to change based on the mode of delivery. However, there are some technical changes that we will deal with below.

• •

Scanning: technical matters

We have mentioned that there are some technical matters to consider when preparing a cover letter that may be scanned by an OCR. Here are some pointers to keep in mind to keep your cover letter scanner-friendly:

• Use familiar type faces (fonts); size should be between 10-14 points.

• Avoid using italics or underlining.

• Sometimes boldface is a problem, so use capital letters instead.

- Avoid shading and graphics, which use horizontal or vertical lines.
- Leave space between letters and lines of text.
- If possible, use a laser printer. A high quality dot matrix printer will likely be scannable as well.
- Print black ink on white paper for best effect.
- Some scanners have difficulty with bullets. If you do use bullets, make sure they are solid, not hollow. If you are submitting your cover letter by e-mail, use an asterisk rather than a bullet.
- Do not staple your cover letter to your resume. By the way, you wouldn't staple them even if you knew they wouldn't be scanned.
- Do not fold your cover letter. This means using large envelopes rather than the standard #10 envelope.

Note: If you are sending your cover letter and resume by e-mail, make sure you are using an ASCII text (most word processing packages are), and have a clear, descriptive title for the subject of your e-mail correspondence.

• •

By template. Sometimes you are asked to respond by completing a template. Most of the data boxes are for objective material such as your job titles or e-mail address. However, many templates offer the opportunity to send a brief text. If capacity is limited, you can send a "quickie" letter like this one:

"My six years of experience in inventory management should be an asset to your firm. I have a firm grasp of JIT, proven skills in organization, logistics and supervision.

"Your firm is of particular interest to me because of your product line and because I want to return to the Chicago area."

Some templates are able to accommmodate a full cover letter. Addresses and salutations are not recommended for a text of this type. Just get to your core message, which is experience, skills, motivation and geographic compatibility.

Databases

Some computer bulletin boards also have a database component. In essence, you can submit your job application information to the database once and then send it to employers in response to specific postings on the bulletin board with a click of a mouse. This situation allows you a proactive role in determining where your information is sent. These firms tend to refer to a resume database, as we soon shall see.

Many databases allow you to change your resume. In that case you can loosen the constraints of the "one-size-fits-all" form by appending a brief note or amending your resume, both of which fit in nicely with using a cover letter.

There are a number of companies that will accept and store your resume in a database. If the database is designed for subscribing employers, your file can then be accessed by an employer seeking certain job-related characteristics. In principle, your file could be accessed by numerous employers, day or night, without any further action on your part. Some databases include a safety feature to prevent your file from being accessed against your wishes—let's say by your current employer.

Databases maintained by employing firms directly hold applicant data only for their own use.

Information from an applicant database is searched when an employer submits a job requisition. Let's say that Someco is seeking a product manager with five years of experience. A job requisition is submitted to the system identifying what skills to search for. The computer is given a set of words and acronyms to look for, perhaps in a given context. That way it can distinguish between, say, Harvard University and Harvard Graphics. The results of the computer search are delivered to the designated official, whether in human resources or a hiring manager. This individual can then call up the applicant files and read them.

If the computer has identified more applicants than the employer wishes to review, s/he can tighten the parameters until the desired number of applicants is identified.

How does this screening process affect you? Let's say that the employer wanted to read 100 resumes in order to invite 10 people to an interview with the goal of hiring one person. If computer searches didn't exist, an employee of Someco would quickly scan the hundreds of resumes it receives each week and put most in the reject pile. Sheer volume would necessitate this. The "yes" and "maybe" piles would be composed of cover letters and resumes that stood out by presenting plausible match with the firm's needs. Human beings are fallible, especially when under stress and time constraints. The computer's ability to scan and store thousands of resumes may mean that your application will get more attention than would be possible in a traditional search.

Advantages of computerized job searches

Where computer search capability does exist, you have these potential advantages:

Timing issues are minimized. Your letters and resumes can be stored for an extended period of time. This is particularly useful if you are interested in a position that is not available at the time your application is sent.

Relaxed space constraints. You can write a longer resume, cover letter or cover letter/resume combination because electronic applicants usually don't need to follow the general one-page rule of paper submissions.

Multiple employers. Electronic submissions to databases can be accessed by many employers, including those you may not have identified yourself.

You could also experience these disadvantages in a computerized applicant search:

Motivation. Your motivation for wanting a particular kind of job with a particular kind of company isn't likely to be "hit" by the computer during an initial search.

Soft skills. Your work ethic and interpersonal skills are harder to convey to a computer than to a person.

Where are we now?

In this chapter, we have seen how the Job Search Club learned to identify a wealth of potential employers, both large and small. By using the two-criteria method, JSC members were able to prioritize their outreach effort and develop mailing lists of a manageable size.

Since the JSC has learned how to write a prototype cover letter as a basis for writing to many potential employers, writing to 100 firms sharing some basic similarity (job type, industry, geography) is not an impossible task.

Chapter 13

∙∙

The Computer-Based Job Search: A New Tool

∙∙

We have discussed the computer job search and its implications for your job search in several chapters of this second edition. Here is a brief summary of where we stand:

On balance, scanning and computer applicant databases are probably to your advantage, especially in terms of outreach to larger firms. Similarly, through databases your file will be accessible to more employers than would have been the case in a traditional search. However, for people who are changing careers or whose main strength is in soft skills, the advantages are less pronounced.

The members of the Job Search Club contemplated what we had learned about the opportunities and challenges presented by computerized job searches and asked some insightful questions.

Anthony wanted to get to the bottom line: "Is this computer job search going to make it harder, easier or just different?" he asked. "The most important thing to understand," I told Anthony, "is that the computer is one more tool for you to use in your job search. It is not a magic pill. It does not replace networking, job fairs and your own outreach efforts. The computer job search adds opportunities to them."

No panacea

It is quite possible that the computer databases will not be the most significant path to interviews for most people for two reasons:

Job growth is most significant in smaller companies for which these systems are not cost-effective and, therefore, not widely used (at least not yet).

The greatest beneficiaries of the computer database system will be people who have easily identifiable, highly attractive characteristics. Most of us are not in that category, because we are starting or restarting careers, changing career paths, or we excel in soft skills areas.

Now let's look at those three important adjectives Anthony mentioned.

Easier. Researching companies and industries can be easier for everyone because of the wealth of material available on the Web. Job search for high-profile individuals is easier because their job skills can score frequent hits because they are easily identified.

Harder. Computer scanning and data storage may mean a slightly different way of massaging your prototype cover letter and using it in partnership with your resume. (See Chapters 7 and 9.)

Different. Seeking a job by computer is different from seeking by paper. However, the difference is not so great that it will stand in your way.

To respond to Anthony's questions: Use the computer tools available to you but don't rely on them. They are not central to your job search in any case.

David seemed a bit concerned about what I had told Anthony. "If the technically skilled, experienced applicants are the prime beneficiaries of computerized data submission, what does that say to someone just graduating college, not to mention a liberal arts major like me?"

"Computerized data submission is still worth pursuing," I told him. Here's why:

There is little or no financial cost. Most databases and bulletin boards charge no fee to job applicants. Even if you don't have a computer, you can have access to such programs through the library and other sources.

It might help. Particularly worth considering are the bulletin boards that focus on your situation, such as career goal or recent college graduate status. Jobweb (http://www.jobweb.org) and Catapult (http://www.jobweb.org/catapult/) are two such sources. Both are under the aegis of the National Association of Colleges and Employers (NACE).

Harry, a seasoned professional seeking to change fields, added a comment and a question. "I can relate your answer to David to my own situation, except for the specific point about recent college graduate bulletin boards," he said. The other seasoned workers looking for a change nodded their heads in agreement. "Let me take you back to your discussion about scanning. If your cover letter is scanned into the computer, fine. But what if it is discarded?"

"Let's think about this together," I suggested to Harry. "There is never a guarantee that your cover letter is going to be read, even if a firm doesn't use a scanner. Because you have developed a good prototype, the time cost of writing your cover letter is minimal. If it is scanned, you win twice. First, you may score more "hits" as the firm's applicant tracking system responds to a hiring requisition. Second, if you pass the first screen, your cover letter will be called up with its partner, your resume. At that point, whether your cover letter is read first or second is really immaterial."

A limitation of these databases is their "one-size-fits-all" approach. You submit your data once and don't know where it's going. That precludes your addressing a particular interest in a specific employer—one of the advantages of a cover letter. However, the opportunity to boost your candidacy through your cover letter remains. The reason is this: Unlike paper resumes, what you submit to a database is not restricted to one page. Therefore, you can submit a cover letter and resume together, a file that will include some of the advantages of a targeted, paper cover letter:

- *Highlighting* and *reframing* aspects of your resume. This gives you more chances to score "hits" at the computer phase of a firm's applicant search.

- Your *motivation* for a type of job, company and industry can and should be stated.

- *Additional information*, such as willingness to relocate, can and should be stated.

If you pass the initial screen, the employer will then take a look at your entire file. At that stage, the cover letter component of your file is likely to be read along with your resume.

Chapter 14

....

...And More
Cover Letters!

....

In the previous chapters, we have discussed how to write a good cover letter and how to utilize modular construction so that you can produce dozens of individualized letters from one prototype text. In addition, we have given examples of letters you might write in a variety of circumstances.

To make our presentation clear, we used a no-frills style of writing. Once you feel comfortable with the basics, you may want to write in a style that better reflects your own personality. To that end, this chapter will show you letters for a variety of situations written in a variety of styles. Please remember that these are samples, not models to be copied verbatim.

Broadcast letter without a resume

1763 Tarheel Lane
Forestree, NC 28163

November 13, 1996

Mr. Theodore Malone
Vice President, Marketing
Wiskbroom, Inc.
Salisbury, North Carolina 28145

Dear Mr. Malone:

As one marketing professional to another, perhaps we can be of assistance to each other. I am looking for my next job and you may need a successful product manager.

You probably want to know why I say "successful." Here are a few examples:

>   I guided a new invention through a thicket of regulatory barriers and initial market indifference. Today, that product is grossing $85 million per year.

>   I managed a children's toy project from market research to distribution in the stores. Profits have been between $15 and $20 million annually for six years.

>   I negotiated an advertising contract that purchased prime time at reduced rates. The product gained national recognition while advertising cost 20 percent less than budgeted.

Marketing is more than a job for me—it is my passion. For that reason, I am being very selective in companies I contact. Wiskbroom, Inc., appeals to me because I admire the simple ingenuity of your products. As your chairman, Lou Van Hustle, said: "With a clean product, you don't have to launder the profits."

If you think there may be a match between your firm and my talents, let's discuss it. I will call you next week.

Sincerely yours,

Allan Kaufner

Allan Kaufner

Cover letter using a networking contact

77 Echo Hill Road
Lincoln, NE 68504

April 19, 1997

Mr. Robert Asebrook
J.R. Dime & Company
4314 Hickory Drive
Seattle, WA 98117

Dear Mr. Asebrook:

We have a friend in common. I was in Omaha last week for my college class reunion and had dinner with your neighbor, Denny Stein. Denny and I were talking shop and I told him about my desire to seek some new professional challenges. Yours was the first name Denny mentioned as a gold mine of information, especially in regard to catalog sales.

I would appreciate the opportunity of meeting with you to explore some ideas about increasing market penetration in the Pacific Northwest. Next month, I will be in Seattle on family business. Will you be my guest for lunch or dinner?

Next week I will call you to see if your crowded calendar allows you to spend some time with me.

Yours truly,

Sidney Podwol

Sidney Podwol

cc: Denny Stein

Cover letter from a consultant

2327 Bustleton St.
Philadelphia, PA 19152

April 10, 1997

Ms. Jean Dagilus
President
Alliance Health Products
444 Washington Drive
Valley Forge, PA 19482

Dear Ms. Dagilus:

I recently heard from one of your employees that Alliance Health Products has decided to computerize several key departments. Many firms experiencing this transition discover that they have intelligent employees who don't know how to use new, sophisticated equipment. How can you make your investment in machines pay off without incurring a major cost for training?

As an experienced computer systems manager now in a private consulting practice, I am available for projects like yours at a reasonable cost.

A brochure indicating my track record in computer utilization and employee training is enclosed. Next week, I will call you to discuss what our next step should be.

Yours truly,

John Sardinas

John Sardinas

Enclosure

A live job lead

93 Summit Ave.
Montvale, NJ 07645

May 8, 1997

Ms. Bobbi Kenney
Business Manager
Invisible Theater Company
123 East 56th Street
New York, NY 10155

Dear Ms. Kenney:

Laura Swenson told me that she resigned recently to move closer to her fiancee. I know that you will miss Laura as a person and as a professional. But the show must go on, so you are probably looking for someone to fill the role Laura played so well as your stage manager. May I suggest my own name for your consideration?

The theater has been my passion since high school. While I have been an amateur actress, managing the stage has been of greater interest over the last five years. It allows me to combine my passion with my penchant for pragmatism. Consider these accomplishments:

- Stage Manager for both low-budget productions like *Insomnia in Syracuse* and high-tech extravaganzas like *Star Jars: Revenge of the Vulcanized Peanut Butter.*
- Managed productions with both amateur crews and unionized crews. The curtain went up on schedule in every case.
- Every stage show I managed came in on or under budget.

Although I enjoy my current job, I am looking for a new challenge. The Invisible Theater, with your imaginary actors and transparent props, is just what I am looking for.

My resume is enclosed. Let's discuss the possibility of my joining your theater group as stage manager. I will call you in a few days to see what you think.

Sincerely,

Julianne Benoit

Julianne Benoit
cc: Laura Swenson

Enclosure

Letter to an executive recruiter

9210 Jeronimo Road
Irvine, CA 92718

July 7, 1997

Ms. Charles Lapidus
Principal
Iona Associates
14 Spruce Place
Menlo Park, CA 94025

Dear Ms. Lapidus:

Iona Associates enjoys a good reputation for matching managerial talent to the needs of your clients, so I wanted you to know that I am actively pursuing my next career challenge.

I earned my MBA from the Wharton School in 1983 and have held progressively more responsible positions in corporate finance. At present I am the treasurer of a Fortune 1000 firm based in the Midwest. Among my accomplishments are a restructuring of debt that reduced our interest payments by 50 percent and a secondary stock offering that raised $150 million without diminishing our stock's market value to current shareholders.

A recent buyout by a foreign-owned firm makes it prudent for me to investigate other opportunities. Of greatest interest to me would be a CFO or treasurer's post in a mid-sized consumer products firm, although financial services or manufacturing might also produce a good fit. My previous assignments have taken me to the four corners of the United States, so I am prepared to relocate almost anywhere.

Because of the sensitivity of my current situation, I must ask you to keep this correspondence in the strictest confidence. I will contact you on Monday, July 14, to see what our next step should be.

Sincerely,

Sheldon Lerner

Sheldon Lerner

Letter to an executive search firm

1324 Kierth Plaza
Omaha, NE 68131

April 16, 1997

Mr. Arnold Michaels
Comsup & Conner
Three Central Park Plaza
Omaha, NE 68102

Dear Mr. Michaels:

Due to a corporate restructuring, I find myself in the job market for the first time in a long while. In addition to my own outreach and networking efforts, I am seeking a good executive search firm to help me connect with the right situation. Your name was given to me by a close friend whom you helped several years ago under similar circumstances.

Until last month, I was the vice president in charge of manufacturing for FLEC, a manufacturer of computer components based in Connecticut. Although we offered an excellent product at a competitive price, FLEC has decided to move manufacturing offshore and place a national of that country in charge. My career until now has been marked by success at every step, beginning with my first assignment on the shop floor 15 years ago. I am certain that both my technical knowledge and managerial ability would make me an asset to at least one of your clients.

Last year I earned more than $150,000 in salary and bonuses. My intent is to find a new position with similar potential.

I will contact you during the week of April 21 to discuss our next step. I am confident that, working together, we can bring this search to a successful conclusion.

Sincerely,

Alexander Apics

Alexander Apics

Cover letter from college grad with work experience

76 West Los Olas Blvd.
Ft. Lauderdale, FL 33301

January 16, 1997

Ms. Juanita Staver
Director of College Relations
Yunge & Olde Associates
14341 NW 53 Avenue
Miami, FL 33014

Dear Ms. Staver:

I am interested in joining the media staff of Yunge & Olde Associates. My interest in this area developed from my summer jobs and my academic studies in communication at the University of Florida. The media role in an advertising agency is critical to its success and I can offer several qualities that would make me an asset to you.

A media planner must be a good researcher and work well under deadlines. In my summer jobs I have proven both characteristics. For example, last year I researched potential end users for a newly developed widget. I uncovered an entire market segment that had not been previously considered. More recently, I was able to meet or beat all deadlines for mutual fund status reports.

I have been selective in identifying advertising agencies to contact. I am attracted to Yunge & Olde for two reasons. First, I was impressed by a story in *Advertising Weekly* that described how your agency attracted the Robber Robot account, which had been with a much larger agency. Second, the fact that your employees can progress from media to account work fits my career plans exactly.

My resume is enclosed. I will be in Miami from February 10-20 and I am eager to meet with you in person. Next week I will call you to see if we can arrange a meeting at that time.

Sincerely,

Scott Elder

Scott Elder

Enclosure

Cover letter from soon-to-be college grad with technical degree

404 Wheeler Dr.
Austin, TX 78722

April 24, 1997

Mr. Sam Bridges
Senior Project Manager
Manufacturing Designs
2741 Westfield Pike
Melville, NY 11747

Dear Mr. Bridges:

As a forthcoming graduate in industrial engineering, I am interested in joining Manufacturing Designs. My interest in your firm was sparked during a series of projects I completed as part of my engineering training. I know you need talented people, so let me tell you why you should consider me for an interview.

Pursuit of excellence: I graduated in the top 5 percent of my engineering class.

Project experience: Through both class assignments and part-time jobs, I demonstrated the ability to be a productive member of technical group project teams.

Understanding your methods: Two of my projects and one research paper dealt with the same production process you utilize for clients—THRUPUT.

ISO 9000: Through APICS and class work, I have mastered the ISO 9000 standards, which will increasingly be of interest to your clients.

What attracts a Texas native like me to Manufacturing Designs? On a personal basis, I am getting married soon and my fiancee lives in New York. In professional terms, I am looking for a firm that has demonstrated the energy and talent for expanding its client list even in the face of an economic slowdown.

I would deeply appreciate the opportunity of visiting Manufacturing Designs, a firm I have admired for several years. Next week, I will call you to see if you can set aside some time to meet with me.

Sincerely,

Harland Tunnel

Harland Tunnel

Enclosure

Cover letter from soon-to-be college grad with business degree

404 Wheeler
Amherst, MA 01003

February 8, 1997

Kevin Johansen
Human Resources Manager
Superior Furniture, Inc.
1732 Furniture Drive
Danbury, CT 06813

Dear Mr. Johansen:

After reading Superior Furniture's homepage on the Internet, I became interested in an entry level management accounting position in one of your 13 case goods manufacturing plants. Having taught myself carpentry, I have developed a working knowledge of furniture manufacturing and have a genuine interest in the furniture industry. As stated in my resume, I will be graduating in May 1997, with a bachelor's degree in business administration.

Recently I wrote an extensive research paper on the furniture industry, arguing that there are many opportunities for expanding markets, especially in the international field. As you are aware, changing trends in consumer demand, process innovation and the rising wages overseas represent opportunities for domestic manufacturing and marketing functions. As I researched the top 10 major furniture manufacturers, I found them all to be successful. However, I became especially excited about Superior Furniture after analyzing your most recent annual report. Your company appears to have a growth strategy foreseeing these trends, giving Superior Furniture a strong competitive edge in the industry.

I have received an outstanding education from the University of Massachusetts and intend to take the Certified Management Accountant (CMA) exam. I believe that my strong work ethic and genuine enthusiasm will be an asset for Superior Furniture's mission-oriented environment.

My resume is enclosed. I would like to arrange for an interview and a tour through one of your plants at some point during March or April. Next week, I will call you to see what our next step should be.

Sincerely,

William J. Rogers

William J. Rogers

Enclosure

Cover letter for career changer

58 Parkview Street
Springfield, MA 01104
(413) 734-4893

April 18, 1997

Tracey Stenkowski
Data for Dollars, Inc.
370 Rodman Street
Chicago, IL 60606

Dear Ms. Stenkowski:

I am interested in joining Data for Dollars, Inc., in client services. Upon investigation of the client service position in your firm, I believe that I can make a substantial contribution to your firm.

The ability to be flexible and adapt to new situations is an integral part of my current position as an underwriter for Disaster Insurance. My daily activities may vary, from evaluating rating structure, to discussing competition in the marketplace, to handling administrative issues with home office personnel. In an increasingly competitive group insurance environment, I have been able to assist two representatives into the "Top 20" sales category, while providing profitable business.

A career in the Info-Scan division of Data for Dollars would be especially appealing to me. It would enable me to combine my interest in market research with my experience in risk analysis. I am particularly impressed by your firm because I perform best in energetic, creative work environments.

I would like an opportunity to discuss career possibilities for me at Data for Dollars. In June, I will be settling near Chicago, so I will be available for work in the near future. I will contact your office on April 25, to see what our next step should be.

Thank you.

Sincerely yours,

Lysondra Hartley

Lysondra Hartley

Enclosure

Broadcast letter responding to a media announcement

1803 Revere Drive
Boston, MA 02116

September 1, 1997

Mr. Len Vassalo
Sales Manager
Alliance Sales
95 Portent Street
Hampshire, MA 01060

Dear Mr. Vassalo:

I recently saw your name in the *Daily Hampshire Gazette.* Congratulations! Achieving increased sales for the third straight year is a great accomplishment, especially in the current economic environment.

As a recent college graduate, I am looking for a growing firm where I can contribute my skills and drive. Perhaps Alliance Sales could benefit from the enthusiasm and business sense that helped me become the number-one sales representative for Fireplace Products last summer.

My interest in Alliance Sales is rooted in several factors. First, your firm demonstrates the aggressive sales philosophy that I deeply admire. Second, I believe that selling intangibles tends to be both challenging and financially rewarding. Third, I attended college in Hampshire County and would like to return there to live.

My resume will show you that I have sales experience, drive and determination. Meeting me in person will convince you that I can apply those talents to Alliance Sales. I will call you in a few days so we can arrange a meeting.

Sincerely yours,

Lucia Aspiro

Lucia Aspiro

Enclosure

Response to a newspaper ad

254 Oser Avenue
Hauppauge, NY 11788

June 1, 1997

Ms. Alise Olde
Vice President, Marketing
Consumerco
7000 Central Highway
Pennsauken, NJ 08109

Dear Ms. Olde:

The Burlington News published a notice indicating that your firm is seeking an experienced market researcher. Although I have responded to the designated box number, I also wanted to touch base with you personally. As the Vice President of Marketing of Consumerco, you can judge better than anyone else if I am a person worth interviewing.

In my six years of professional market research at Consumer Preference Associates (CPA), I have developed the very skills you need in your department:

> Researched consumer preferences among products of different colors, services with different names and slogans of varied pitch.

> Analyzed data from scanners to identify the compatibility of a client's syrup with a hot-selling waffle mix.

> Advised clients to avoid linking their product with a popular TV program. A competitor linked with that program and suffered a serious loss of market share.

> Wrote survey plans, questionnaires and reports that were praised as user friendly and highly perceptive.

Although I have enjoyed my experience at CPA, I am excited about the possibility of joining Consumerco. *Marketing Monthly* magazine mentioned your firm as a leader in using market research to identify new markets for existing products. That is a challenge I would especially relish.

My resume gives a more detailed picture of the projects I have undertaken and the methods I used. I will contact your office next week to see what our next step should be.

Sincerely,

Michelle Jillian

Michelle Jillian

Enclosure

Response to a "blind" ad

11933 Washington Boulevard
Culver City, CA 90232

June 20, 1996

P.O. Box 170
Fairfax, VA 22031

In regard to your notice in the June 19 *Hampshire Gazette*, this is what I can offer your firm:

• Five years selling experience for a hospital supply firm.

• Expanded client base by 40% through persistent effort and excellent service.

• Ninety percent (90%) of my clients renewed annual contracts.

• Traveled throughout large territory, but managed time well.

Result: a broader and deeper market.

Does this sound like the person you need? If it is, I am eager to speak with you.

Sincerely,

Brenna O'Neil

Brenna O'Neil

Enclosure

Follow-up response to a "blind" ad

7432 Prospect St.
Northampton, MA 01060

April 29, 1997

P.O. Box XYZ
Manchester-Maven Gazette
Manchester, NH 03868

I am writing to express my continued interest in the position described in the *Manchester-Maven Gazette* of April 15. Deciding whom to interview from among many applicants is surely a difficult task, so it is easy to understand why I haven't heard from you.

My employers have consistently evaluated me highly for performance, energy and innovation—the very qualities you are seeking. A copy of my original correspondence is enclosed. May I look forward to hearing from you?

Yours truly,

John Johnstone

John Johnstone

Enclosures

Letter requesting informational meeting

986 Linden Boulevard
Elkhart, IN 46515

October 3, 1995

Ms. Regina Coleman
Vice President, Human Resources
Crashco Insurance
8213 Arboretum Boulevard
Austin, TX 78759

Dear Ms. Coleman:

Because my wife has been transferred by her company, I am investigating opportunities in the Austin area. Could you spend 10 to 15 minutes with me to discuss employment opportunities in the insurance industry? Your insights and suggestions might ease the transition process our two-career family is currently facing.

A few words about me. For 15 years, I have built a career with insurance firms in Boston, Chicago and Denver. My responsibilities have been to assess risk for increasingly complicated and novel projects. Risk management is of particular interest to me based on my past success. However, product development or group product marketing might also be logical next steps.

Your time is very precious and I promise to safeguard it. I will call you next week with the hope that you can offer me the benefit of your advice.

Sincerely,

Jerry Goldin

Jerry Goldin

Letter requesting informational meeting citing a common friend

2843 Faunce Street
Philadelphia, PA 19154

October 13, 1996

Mr. John Goldin
Senior Financial Analyst
Profitco
Five Mariner Parkway
Haverton, PA 19067

Dear Mr. Goldin:

A mutual friend, Beth Ginzi, suggested that I contact you. Beth knows that I am looking to take my next career step and she said that you were a fountain of information.

By way of background, I have a dozen years of experience in the credit field. However, I would like to learn more about asset-based lending, and your input could be invaluable in that area.

I know how tight your schedule must be. Next week I will call you to see if a brief meeting can be arranged.

Sincerely,

Al Levine

Al Levine

Letter requesting industry information

353 Augusta Street
Portland, ME 04104

September 10, 1996

Mr. Isidore Fine
Vice President, Systems
Macromaid, Inc.
Three Wellington Place
Seattle, WA 98118

Dear Mr. Fine:

Would you be willing to spend a little time with me on the telephone? I will be moving to the Seattle area soon and am inquiring about employment opportunities for information systems specialists.

At present, I manage a project team with Complico in Portland, Maine. In addition to a demonstrated expertise with a variety of mainframe systems, I have shown the ability to guide a group of technically minded people in producing a useful end product for results-oriented managers. Because Complico is now downsizing following a merger, I am exploring opportunities in Seattle, where I attended college.

In the hope that you can share a few ideas with me, I will call you on Monday, November 18. My resume is enclosed on a strictly FYI basis.

Sincerely yours,

Gregory Gall
Gregory Gall

Enclosure

Broadcast letter from a noncitizen

3714 Dankel Drive
Rancho Cordova, CA 95670

July 7, 1996

Mr. Daniel Johnson
President
West Coast Widgets, Inc.
425 Pacific View Drive
Mountain Peak, CA 94039

Dear Mr. Johnson:

Does your department anticipate the need for marketing expertise in the Pacific Rim? As a bilingual (Chinese-English) graduate of the Buckland School MBA program, perhaps I can be of service.

A little bit about my background may be in order. I was raised in Taiwan as the oldest son of a family deeply involved with product distribution. After graduating from the University of Taipei, I spent two years planning the logistics of my family's trucking business and two years working for the Commerce Minister. Both experiences enabled me to develop good business sense in addition to valuable contacts. At the Buckland School, I strengthened my business credentials by learning about business and trade from an American perspective.

An article in *The Economist* indicates that you are exploring trade with the Pacific Rim but have not yet developed commercial ties to the area. May I suggest myself as the way to fill your need for expertise in this area?

I am available on either a one-year or long-term basis. Because of my F-1 visa status, the first option would present no difficulty for you in terms of U.S. immigration policy.

One thing I learned about American business culture is the value of being proactive. I will contact you next week to see if a meeting can be arranged at your convenience.

Sincerely,

Chi-Ming Ho

Chi-Ming Ho

Enclosure

Follow-up to a job interview

845 S. Michigan Ave.
Chicago, IL 60605

April 26, 1996

Mr. Mark Schewe
Principal
Schewe Associates
1436 Twin City Center
St. Paul, MN 54144

Dear Mark:

Thursday, April 25, was one of the most impressive days of my professional life. Meeting with you, Jack Wolfe and Charlie Malone, I spent the day with three of the best business planners I have ever met. Now I can understand why Schewe Associates is so highly regarded.

Frankly, I hope that you were equally impressed with me.

Sincerely yours,

Kathleen Campbell

Kathleen Campbell

Follow-up to a job interview—reviewing selling points

1739 N. Aberdeen Street
Amherst, MA 01002

May 7, 1997

Ms. Corona Shipman
Rum & Nehan
1924 Harbor Road
Brighton, MA 02135

Dear Ms. Shipman:

I want to thank you again for the opportunity to interview with you on January 9. Our discussion about a possible position for me with Rum & Nehan was both interesting and informative.

As you assess the interview, I hope you will agree that I offer the three qualities you need most in the person you are seeking: intellectual curiosity, communication skills and proven ability to deal constructively with client problems. In addition, many of the challenges I have dealt with at Currentco closely parallel those you are experiencing at Rum & Nehan.

You indicated that you prefer not to receive phone calls from job applicants and I certainly understand that. I hope that I will hear from you about a follow-up interview in the near future.

Sincerely,

Rebecca Benson

Rebecca Benson

Rejecting a job offer

3517 West Street
Amherst, MA 01002

March 21, 1997

Mr. David Partson
Sandersen & Co.
1776 Heritage Parkway
Woburn, MA 01801

Dear Mr. Partson:

It was nice speaking with you yesterday, but it was also a little sad. After meeting with you and other members of the Sandersen team during the last semester, it was difficult to turn down an offer to join your firm.

To confirm our conversation, I am honored by your offer of employment. However, I must decline it because I have concluded that starting my career with another firm is a more appropriate match for me.

Thank you for your time and consideration.

Sincerely yours,

Leanne McGregory

Leanne McGregory

Withdrawing from further consideration

1415 Comiskey Street
Itasca, IL 60143

July 20, 1997

Ms. Sarah Woodbury
Vice President, Marketing
Demographics, Inc.
3713 Hoosier Boulevard
Indianapolis, IN 46268

Dear Sarah:

I deeply appreciate the time and consideration you have given me in our recent discussions about a market research position at Demographics, Inc. The people I met were dedicated and talented. They bring pride to our profession.

As you were aware, two other firms have also been interviewing me for career opportunities with them. Infodata offered me an interesting opportunity and I accepted it yesterday.

Please withdraw my name from further consideration by Demographics, Inc. I hope our paths will cross again, perhaps at a marketing convention.

Yours truly,

Catherine Debevec

Catherine Debevec

Letter of resignation

6901 East 21st Street
Wichita, KS 67206

May 8, 1997

Ms. Dorothy Gin
Director of Marketing
PALCO Health Services
44 Earp Street
Wichita, KS 67208

Dear Dorothy:

This will confirm our discussion of yesterday in which I advised you of my resignation from PALCO Health Services. My three years at PALCO have been a wonderful experience, but I feel the time has come to move on to new challenges.

The latest possible date for me to leave is June 30, although I prefer to leave by June 1. Please let me know your preferences in this matter. In either event, I will make sure that my area of responsibility remains in solid working order for my successor.

Sincerely,

Judith Bluestone

Judith Bluestone

cc: Mr. Edward Rawlins

Letter thanking people who helped you in the job search

76 Prospect Street
St. Paul, MN 54144

January 15, 1997

Ms. Dorothy Pokros
Senior Financial Analyst
Heavyduty Manufacturing Company
17 Nuts & Bolts Drive
Iowa City, IA 52333

Dear Dorothy,

I want to share some great news with you. Last week, I was offered a position as a financial analyst with Supercom, Inc., in Cedar Rapids. Yesterday, I accepted the offer.

The insights and ideas you shared with me this past October played a big part in getting me through the interview process. I deeply appreciate everything you have done to help me launch my career.

Thank you.

Sincerely,

David McGrath

David McGrath

Epilogue

···

A Final Review

···

This book is designed to help you get a good job. A cover letter that adds value to your resume is an important part of your job-search effort. The importance of a cover letter grows in a tight economy. Dozens or even hundreds of people may apply for each good job opening. A cover letter that shows what you can do for the prospective employer and what motivates you to have an interest in a particular job can make you stand out above your competitors. We have shown how to present yourself well to an employer even when you are not an obvious candidate for the job, based on past work experience. Your cover letter should be built around four key paragraphs:

- An opening that describes why you are writing.

- A "why you should interview me" paragraph, which indicates skills you have that the employer needs and supports your statements with examples.

- A "why I want to work for you" paragraph that explains your attraction to the job, the firm and/or industry.

- A closing that indicates you will initiate follow-up.

This book is written for the thinking job-seeker. We emphasized quality cover letters and not mere letters of transmittal or amorphous pleas for a job. That is one reason for the chapters on research and networking. A thinking job-seeker also realizes that landing his or her next job interview will probably require more than one letter. How do you deal with the twin factors of quantity and quality? Our solution is modular construction based on a well-written prototype. Cover letters don't operate alone. For that reason, we included a chapter on making your letter a powerful partner with your resume. Of course, your letter needs to be sent to someone in particular, by name. Identifying that person was the subject of Chapters 11 and 12.

There is one factor we did not dwell on: perseverance. Looking for a job can be emotionally draining. More often than not, your efforts will not result in an interview. The ultimate goal is getting a job you really want. Along the road, you are likely to experience disappointments. Those who give up the search will pay the price of an unsatisfactory job—or no job at all. But those who persevere intelligently in the face of frustration will enjoy the fruits of satisfying employment. I would be interested in learning how your job search develops. You can write to me at:

Richard Fein
Director of Placement
School of Management
University of Massachusetts
Amherst, MA 01003

Appendix

Resource List

Career planning

The Career Decisions Planner: When to Move, When to Stay, and When to Go Out on Your Own, Joan Lloyd, John Wiley and Sons, Inc., 1992.

Career Planning Today: Hire Me!, 2nd edition, C. Randall Powell, Kendall/Hunt Publishing Co., 1990.

It's Never Too Late: 150 Men & Women Who Changed Their Careers, Robert K. Otterbourg, Barron's, 1993.

Joyce Lain Kennedy's Career Book, 2nd edition, co-authored by Dr. Darryl Laramore, VGM Career Horizons, 1993.

Occupational Outlook Handbook (1990-91 edition), Bureau of Labor Statistics, U.S. Department of Labor, U. S. Government Printing Office, 1990.

Where to Start Career Planning—Essential Resource Guide for Career Planning and Job Hunting, 8th edition (1991-1993), Carolyn Lloyd Lindquist, Diane June Miller, Cornell University, 1991.

Breakaway Careers: The Self-Employment Resource for Freelancers, Consultants and Corporate Refugees, Bill Radin, Career Press, Inc., 1994.

Part-Time Careers, Joyce Hadley, Career Press, Inc., 1993.

What is a job like?

Careers for Foreign Language Aficionados and Other Multilingual Types, H. Ned Seelye, J. Laurence Day, VGM Career Horizons, NTC Publishing Group, 1992.

Careers in Public Accounting: A Comprehensive Comparison of the Top Ten Firms, 3rd edition, James C. Emerson, Professional Services Review, 1991.

Commercial Banking: A TRS Industry Profile, Crimson & Brown Associates, Inc., 1991.

Financial Planning: A Career Profile, International Board of Standards and Practices for Certified Financial Planners, Inc. (IBCFP), 1989.

Getting Into Money: A Career Guide, Cheri Fein, Ballantine Books, 1988.

Insurance: A TRS Industry Profile, Crimson & Brown Associates, Inc., 1991.

Jobs for English Majors and Other Smart People, 3rd edition, John L. Munschauer, Peterson's Guides, Inc., 1991.

Liberal Arts Jobs: What They Are and How to Get Them, Burton Jay Nadler, Peterson's Guides, Inc., 1989.

Making It In Advertising: An Insider's Guide to Career Opportunities, Leonard Mogel, Collier Books, MacMillan Publishing Company, 1993.

Opportunities in Accounting Careers, Martin H. Rosenberg, VGM Career Horizons, 1991.

Opportunities in Engineering Careers, Nicholas Basta, VGM Career Horizons, 1990.

Opportunities in Information Systems Careers, Douglas B. Hoyt, VGM Career Horizons, 1991.

Careers in the nonprofit sector

Careers For Dreamers & Doers: A Guide to Management Careers in the Nonprofit Sector, Lilly Cohen and Dennis R. Young, The Foundation Center, 1989.

Finding a Job in the Nonprofit Sector, William Wade, The Taft Group, 1991.

Identifying potential employers

The American Almanac of Jobs and Salaries, 4th edition, John W. Wright and Edward J. Dwyer, Avon Books, 1990.

America's Fastest Growing Employers: The Complete Guide to Finding Jobs With Over 700 of America's Hottest Companies, Carter Smith, Bob Adams, Inc., 1992.

America's Corporate Families: The Billion Dollar Directory, Vols. 1 & 2, Dun's Marketing Services, 1996.

American Export Register, Thomas International Publishing Company, 1996.

Business Organizations, Agencies and Publications Directory, Sandra MacRitchie, Gale Research, Inc., 1990.

Consultants and Consulting Organizations Directory, 10th edition, Janice McLean, Gale Research, Inc., 1990.

Directory of American Firms Operating in Foreign Countries, 11th edition, 3 vols., Juvenal L. Angel, World Trade Academy Press, Inc., 1996.

Directory of Corporate Affiliations, National Register Publishing Company, 1996.

Directory of Foreign Firms Operating in the United States, Simon & Schuster, 1995.

Directory of Foreign Manufacturers in the United States, Georgia State University Business Press, Atlanta, 1993.

Directory of Leading U.S. Export Management Companies, 3rd edition, Bergano Book Co., Fairfield, Conn., 1991.

Information Industry Directory: An International Guide to Organizations, Systems and Services Involved in the Production and Distribution of Information in Electronic Form, 15th edition, 1995, Gale Research, Inc., 2 vols.

Emerson's Directory of Leading U.S. Accounting Firms, 2nd edition, Professional Services Review, 1990.

Hoover's Handbook: Profiles of Over 500 Major Corporations, Gary Hoover, Alta Campbell and Patrick J. Spain, The Reference Press, Inc., 1994.

How To Get A Job In Europe: The Insider's Guide, Robert Sanborn, Surrey Books, Inc., 1991.

National Directory of Corporate Public Affairs, Columbia Books, Washington, D.C., 1996.

The 100 Best Companies To Sell For, Michael David Harkavy and the Philip Lief Group, John Wiley & Sons, Inc., 1989.

Peterson's Job Opportunities for Business & Liberal Arts Graduates, 8th edition, Peterson's Guides, Inc. 1992.

Peterson's Job Opportunities for Engineering, Science and Computer Graduates, 1992, 13th edition, Peterson's Guides, Inc., 1991.

Poor's Register of Corporations, Directors, and Executives, Annual, 3 vols., Standard & Poor's Corporation, 1996.

Standard Directory of Advertisers (Advertiser Red Book), Annual, National Register Publishing Company, 1990.

Training & Development Organizations Directory, 5th edition, Janice McLean, editor, Gale Research, Inc., 1990.

Researching Your Way to a Good Job, Karmen Crowther, John Wiley & Sons, 1993.

World Wide Branch Locations of Multinational Companies, David S. Hoope, editor, Gale Research, Detroit, 1994.

Some ideas on job search

Electronic Job Search Revolution: Win With New Technology That's Reshaping Today's Job Market, Joyce Lain Kennedy, Thomas J. Morrow, John Wiley & Sons, Inc., 1994.

High Impact Telephone Networking for Job Hunters: Who To Call, What To Say, How To Project A Positive Image, How To Turn Contacts Into Job Offers, Howard Armstrong, Bob Adams, Inc., 1992.

Information Interviewing—What It Is and How To Use It In Your Career, Martha Stoodley, M.S., MFCC, Garnett Park Press, 1990.

Resumes! Resumes! Resumes!, 2nd edition, Career Press Editors, Career Press, 1995.

Take This Job and Leave It: How to Get Out of a Job You Hate and Into a Job You Love, Bill Radin, Career Press, Inc., 1993.

The Smart Woman's Guide to Resumes and Job Hunting, 3rd edition, Julie Adair King and Betsy Sheldon, Career Press, Inc., 1995.

The Smart Woman's Guide to Networking, Joyce Hadley and Betsy Sheldon, Career Press, Inc., 1995.

The Smart Woman's Guide to Interviewing and Salary Negotiation, 2nd edition, Julie Adair King, Career Press, Inc., 1995.

Your First Resume, 4th edition, Ron Fry, Career Press, Inc., 1996.

Your First Interview, 3rd edition, Ron Fry, Career Press, Inc., 1996.

Some sources for using a computer in your job search

Electronic Resume Revolution, Joyce Lain Kennedy, John Wiley & Sons, 1993.

Electronic Job Search Revolution, 2nd edition, Joyce Lain Kennedy and Thomas J. Morrow, John Wiley & Sons, 1995.

Finding a Job on the Internet, Alfred and Emily Glossbrenner, McGraw-Hill, 1995.

Starting a career

First Job: A New Grad's Guide to Launching Your Business Career, Richard Fein, John Wiley & Sons, 1992.

From Campus to Corporation, 2nd edition, Stephen Strasser, Ph.D., and John Sena, Ph.D., Career Press, Inc., 1993.

The New Professional—Everything You Need To Know For A Great First Year on The Job, Ed Holton, Peterson's Guides, Inc., 1991.

Your First Job, 2nd edition, Ron Fry, Career Press, Inc., 1996.

Index